The Shadow of Cliff College

By

Joe Brice

Originally Entitled
SAVED AND SENT

ISBN 0-88019-172-4

Schmul Publishing Co., Inc.
Wesleyan Book Club   Salem, Ohio
1985

Printed by
Old Paths Tract Society Inc.
Shoals, Indiana 47581

By the Same Author

———

PENTECOST
THE CROWD FOR CHRIST

THIS BOOK
ABOUT THE WORK SHE LOVES
IS GRATEFULLY DEDICATED TO
MISS DOUGLAS,
TO WHOM SEVERAL GENERATIONS OF
CLIFF STUDENTS, AND I
PARTICULARLY, OWE AN
INCALCULABLE DEBT

CONTENTS

CHAP.		PAGE
I.	I CAME TO CLIFF	II
II.	THE COLLEGE OF THE UNPRIVILEGED	16
III.	ALL FOR EVANGELISM	21
IV.	INAUGURAL	29
V.	TO THE WORK!	33
VI.	THE TRADITION COMES ALIVE	38
VII.	DAY OF EVANGELISM	43
VIII.	WHAT MANNER OF MEN?	50
IX.	THROUGH CLIFF TO THE MINISTRY	57
X.	CLIFF OVERSEAS	64
XI.	SOULWINNERS ALL	70
XII.	EVANGELICAL TROUBADOURS	76
XIII.	SALVATION AT THE SEASIDE	81
XIV.	TOLD ROUND THE CAMP FIRE	86
XV.	PROVISION	92

I

I CAME TO CLIFF

> " Blessed be the day when I began
>   A pilgrim for to be,
> And thrice more blessed be the man
>   Who thereto movéd me,"

FATHER was always unwell and we were desperately poor. I was the eldest of ten children, and I shared most of the hardship.

Throughout my boyhood our life was a scramble for bread. We were all involved in it. Mother sewed and took in washing ; the rest of us earned as soon as possible. Ill-health kept me from school till I was eight, but I was not too ill to earn, even at six. My first paid labour was traffic with a pawnshop for all our neighbours.

I have been told since that there were periods of relief ; but they did not last long enough to impress me. All I can remember is the interminable scramble, and mother's pathetic effort to hide the facts. The most vivid memories of my childhood are free meals. Through several winters we walked two miles for charity breakfasts, and seven Christmas mornings in succession several of us shared " The Robin's Breakfast " with the poorest children in the town.

Before we were ten years old, my brother and I worked on the streets from six o'clock till nine every morning, every dinner-hour, and every evening till nine o'clock, except on Sundays, vending newspapers. On my thirteenth birthday, I passed a very nominal " labour examination " and left school. Then began an even grimmer struggle against poverty. For a year I was a full-timer on the streets, then, after a few months in a factory which I left in disgrace, I worked for several years in the coal-mine, and finally in a foundry.

Some of my memories will never be written : I buried them in my mother's grave. In any case, they would seem incredible to those who have known only the saved half of my life. Suffice it to say that I and all about me desperately needed the saving power of real religion.

But for all I knew about sin, my own and others, I had no inclination to religion, nor was I vitally influenced by it. One good soul claims that, out of sympathy with my mother, she took me to Sunday School when I was two, but I have no memory of it. There was a vague tradition of former godliness on my father's side, and I inherited a lot of old-fashioned hymns and tunes that made no perceptible moral difference. For several months I sang in a church choir at sixpence a Sunday ; but I was ejected before the ritual had chance to work. These things apart, I had no contact with organized religion, nor did I desire any—the church folk seemed to live in an alien sphere.

I went on with my unwholesome ways till within a few weeks of my sixteenth birthday, conscious only, though in a man's way, of sin's power and its doom, and utterly ignorant of vital inward religion.

A few fervent Primitive Methodist miners were the first to show me the secret of personal salvation ; but, strangely enough, it was not among the Methodists that I found life and peace through believing. Captain Richards, former Candidates Secretary of the Church Army, led me to Christ in an Anglican mission-hall, at the end of a remarkable harvest-festival service. He led me to Christ without knowing it, for he was taken Home to God before my conversion seemed significant enough to report ; but, while that good man was preaching saving grace in the simplest terms, I yielded my life to the Saviour and dimly realized the blessedness of forgiveness.

It will never be possible for me to tell all the meaning of that event for my life. It is simple truth to say that when the Lord Jesus saved me, He redeemed my life from destruction. Blessed be His Name for ever !

I cannot say that my apprehension of the Saviour was all joy. There was an element of unhappiness entailed, for at once I was made to see both the necessity to witness and my own incapacity for it. I was very ignorant of the things of God and I found it very hard to learn. I did not know how to begin to study. My first efforts in Bible-study were painful and disappointing ; and I had no other books. It is hard to realize, as I write amid hundreds of books, that I once walked five miles for a cheap second-hand copy of Oliver's *Synopsis*.

My first helper and encourager was Eli Hammonds, a

miner and one of the godliest men I have ever known ; a member of the mission in which I was converted and a lay-reader in the Church of England. He told me he thought my spiritual experience ought to be grounded in understanding, and gave me a copy of Frances Ridley Havergal's *Kept for the Master's Use*—the first book I ever read through, a feat which, under all circumstances, I regard as the best achievement of my early Christian life.

My friend persevered with me. He tutored me in the sayings and parables of Jesus ; and in a few months, greatly daring, he allowed me to give the message in his service at a little mission-hall two miles away. It was a pathetic effort, but it confirmed my desire to proclaim the grace of Christ revealed in me. Yet I had no confidence whatever in myself, and not the least ground for thinking that I should ever be able to preach acceptably.

Ten months after my conversion, God called me to the ministry, and he over-ruled my inward protest with fiery words from John's Gospel—" Ye have not chosen me, but I have chosen you, and ordained you, that ye should go forth and bear fruit, and that your fruit should remain."

Normally, such a call would be welcomed with joy unspeakable. Being consciously and patently inadequate, I was afraid and unhappy ; and I did not declare the matter to a soul. But God intervened.

One collector among the many who called at our house every Saturday for deferred payments, was a Methodist local preacher. He was a simple, kindly, helpful man ; and one night as we walked his round, I told him all my hopes and fears. By way of answer and encouragement he told me about Cliff College, and particularly about the great man who was then its Principal.

I regard Samuel Chadwick's story, told by my local-preacher friend, as the turning point of my life. Perhaps it can never mean to another soul what it meant, and still means, to me ; but to me, a needy, eager, ignorant disciple of Jesus, it was an answer from heaven.

George Jayes told me that Samuel Chadwick was born in a back street in Burnley. There was not a blade of grass, a tree or a flower in the whole area. It hummed with the noise of factories from morning till night. The only playground was the gutter, and when you were not in the living-room you were in the bedroom.

He was a half-timer at the mill when he was eight, and he had finished with schools when he was eleven. In view of the work that lay before him, there seemed to be no sense in the way he had to tread. But once, when he was brooding over the privations of his early life, God said to him : " He humbled thee, and suffered thee to hunger, that He might make thee know that man doth not live by bread alone, but by every word that proceedeth out of the mouth of the Lord."

He was converted when he was ten, and called to preach when he was fifteen. He found it as hard as I was finding it to fit himself for the preaching of the Gospel ; and the nights of his frail youth, after long days in the mill, were spent laboriously acquiring the elements of knowledge. Toiling through these midnights, without help or guide, there was kindled within him a boundless sympathy with consecrated working lads who longed to improve their education for the Kingdom's sake. He learned then how to " get alongside " the unprivileged, and by-and-by God gave him the opportunity to do it at Cliff.

My friend told me numerous stories of Chadwick's amazing ministries in Clydebank and Leeds, before he was elected to Cliff. The record thrilled me. It was an answer of God to me.

I began to read " Joyful News " ; and, within a few months, like thousands of others who never saw him, I knew Samuel Chadwick perfectly well through his remarkable leaders and letters. And I knew that he was a warrior-saint, a man of God, and a great human, full of sympathy and full of humour ; but his sovereign charm for me was the gracious capacity for helping unprivileged lads.

Imagine the impact of that story upon my soul ! By it God showed me His path for me ; and on the authority of that conviction, and not on account of any scruples about the Anglican Church, which I shall love for ever, I began to seek fellowship with the Methodists.

By the gracious help of the ministers and several local-preachers, especially Tom Somerfield, I was sent to evening classes and otherwise fitted for a place on the Methodist " Plan ". There were more facilities for unprivileged lads in the Methodist Church, and I was soon engrossed in training and service. All the time my heart was set on getting to Chadwick's College. I knew it was the door of hope for me. And as soon as I had fulfilled the conditions of membership and preaching experience, I applied for entrance.

It was impossible to pay fees. A friend gave me £5 which was all I could offer ; but Cliff accepted me on the recommendation of my faithful encouragers, and at last I arrived at the College, with eight shillings in my pocket, a heart full of hope, and the crude conviction that Samuel Chadwick was the man to see me through to where God wanted me to be. He had gone the same way before me.

II

THE COLLEGE OF THE UNPRIVILEGED

CLIFF began as " The Joyful News Mission," at Rochdale in 1884. Its founder was that intrepid apostle of the common people, Thomas Champness. He, like Wilson Carlile, Grattan Guinness and others, shared the evangelistic inspiration which first manifested itself in the heart of William Booth. It was a Spirit-born impulse to reach the masses with the Gospel.

Champness, like Booth and Carlile, saw that the masses would be reached most easily and quickly by an order of evangelists raised from among themselves, an order of godly men, able to speak their plain straightforward simple language, and fraternize with the common people for their salvation.

Under the influence of Moody and Müller, Champness felt compelled to create such an order within the Methodist Church ; but the leaders of Methodism were not yet in a mind to implement the vision. Yet God fulfilled His will in another way.

In the early 'eighties, a revival began in Lancashire. Part of its issue was the great Manchester Mission. Another part was a wonderful work of grace in the Methodist Churches of East Lancashire under the preaching of the new district missionary, Thomas Champness.

In the midst of this revival, Champness wrote in his diary, " Letter from President respecting a new paper, and asking me to go over and see him. Find they want me to edit ! ! ! " The idea of the paper in question was first expressed by several laymen of the district to which the witness of Champness had brought the blessedness of revival. Like General Booth's *War Cry*, which had begun three years earlier, it was to be devoted solely to the interests of evangelism. The need for such a paper was manifest, and several Methodist leaders, notably Charles Garrett and Dr. Osborn, were eager to begin it.

Thomas Champness was fifty, and absolutely innocent of

journalistic experience, but he was willing to undertake the task of editorship on two conditions : " No pay, and my own master." Charles Garrett and Dr. Osborn, however, insisted that he must take a salary and have a sub-editor. There was deadlock ; and Garrett wrote, " It's no use. Let me know how much you are out of pocket ; I will pay you and we must give up the project."

Champness could not give up the project, since he had undertaken it by divine command and not by choice. It was a call, and the more he prayed the deeper became the sense of call. He could not turn back.

He did not turn back. He and his wife put their meagre personal resources behind the paper. They and their friend, Josiah Mee, prayed for a title ; and though many derided the project, the paper appeared on February 22nd, 1883.

The paper contained news of revival, stories of remarkable conversions, answers to prayers, articles by Methodist leaders, including a plea for evangelism by Hugh Price Hughes, and a long report of the opening of Manchester Mission.

The venture was heroic, and the success was embarrassing. Copies could not be printed fast enough. Within a month Champness wrote in his diary, " We have sold thirty thousand. *Te Deum laudamus.*" Yet his greatest joy was not the extent of its circulation, but of its blessing.

The paper provided Champness with an army of sympathisers and helpers. It did more. At the end of his first year as editor he found that he had been growing rich unawares. All he had was the Lord's, and he prayed for guidance in the use of this unexpected profit from the paper. Then the wish of his life became a conviction, and during their morning watch, early in 1884, he and his wife agreed to receive two unprivileged lads into their home for training in evangelistic work. He would take revenge upon life for his own difficult beginnings, and, at the same time, send prophets to the common people. Thus, " The Joyful News Mission " was established.

By 1886 there were twenty-five young men in training, and the capacity of the manse was taxed to the utmost. By 1889 it was necessary for the Mission to seek separate quarters, and the household prayed for guidance. The answer soon came. Just outside Rochdale there was a roomy old mansion called Castleton Hall. There were large rooms, extensive gardens, and commodious stabling. It was within easy reach of the town, and yet quite private, ideal both for evangelism and study. Champness had not dared to hope to possess it, yet at length God made it his. The Mission took possession of Castleton Hall in July, 1889. The Methodist Conference in the same month freed Mr. Champness from the itinerancy, so that he might give his whole time to the training of evangelists. Soon Castleton Hall was filled with evangelists in the making.

An evangelist had to be of heroic mould to suit Champness. When a man applied for training, he was frankly told that the administration was autocratic and the conditions were spartan. The tests were rigorous, but consecrated young men crowded into the service of the Mission; and Champness gathered around himself a magnificent band of young soul-winners. The early story thrills with epics of evangelistic enterprise. His men went with the Gospel through the length and breadth of the land; and some to other lands. They preached full salvation in the language of the common people and God gloriously honoured their witness.

Before Champness retired, he had sent forth over seven hundred evangelists to all parts of the world, some as missioners, others as ministers, missionaries and lay-preachers. Wherever they went they brought the flame of love for the common people which Champness had inspired, and they led thousands of souls to Christ.

When it became necessary for Champness to retire through ill-health, it was found that God had raised up able men to succeed him—men of the same faith and devotion. Samuel Chadwick, who was then exercising a remarkable evangelistic ministry in Leeds, was made the editor of *Joyful News*, and Thomas Cook, who for over twenty years has been a Connexional Evangelist and a great winner of souls, was appointed as director of the Training Home.

"God buries his workman, but carries on his work." In nothing has the favour of God to Cliff been more plainly shown than in the provision of men to carry on its traditions in faith and evangelism. The work requires a special type of leader. He must combine the passion of the evangelist with the skill of the teacher and the ability of the administrator. Humanly speaking, Cliff has impossible traditions; God alone, in wisdom and grace has maintained the succession and maintained it in triumph.

Champness lived by faith. He would not beg, and he would not run into debt. He accepted no fees, and he refused to take collections. The work was founded upon a covenant of prayer. Champness prayed in simple trust, believing that so long as the Lord meant the work to go on the means would be provided, and that when they ceased it would be a sign that the Lord had other plans. The work has lived ever since by the prayer of faith, and the story of Cliff is a pageant of providence.

Cook's first task was to find a new home for the Mission. Once more, the good hand of God was upon his servants. The Rev. H. T. Smart was present at a Methodist quarterly meeting at Bakewell, and casually remarked that the Joyful News Mission needed new quarters, when a member of the meeting told him of a missionary college which was vacant. It was situated on a hillside immortalised by W. E. Watson, beneath Curbar Edge, overlooking the beautiful Derwent Valley. Thomas Cook immediately went to see the building, and soon it was secured for his work. Within a few months it was reconditioned and ultimately opened free of debt. From then till now there has never been a debt upon the place. God honours the original covenant of prayer.

One could tell many stories of the hand of God manifested in magnificent provision for the needs of the place and its work. One who knew the work from the beginning often said. " Every bit of Cliff represents some romance of Providence. Every stick and stone and yard of ground has been prayed into our possession for the glory of God in the salvation of souls." And, as the providence of God has not failed, neither has the faithfulness of His servants to the original charter. When Cook died prematurely, Samuel Chadwick became Principal of the College as well as editor of the paper. He maintained magnificently the work and witness of Thomas Cook and Thomas Champness. When Chadwick died in 1932, John Broadbelt, with an incomparable experience of central mission work, succeeded him; and to-day, as from the beginning, Cliff College exists to train the sons of the poor as evangelists to the masses.

Working youths who are saved and determined to preach the Gospel, enter the College, and for a year undergo a simple but strenuous course in the English Bible and all subjects relevant to the necessities of effective evangelism. Thomas Champness shaped his programme of training by the rule that there are three essentials in the equipment of an evangelist: the Pentecostal experience; an experimental knowledge of the Word of God; and the ability to preach the Gospel to the masses intelligibly and with acceptance.

The teaching programme of Cliff is still ordered by that rule; and admittance to Cliff is still governed by the terms of the original charter. Men are admitted without any stipulated fee; and no man is refused on the ground of poverty, as no man is admitted merely on account of the ability to pay. At the end of the course some of the students remain on the evangelistic staff of the College; some become lay missioners with other organisations; some go to the mission-field abroad; a goodly number enter the various ministries, and a few return to their secular vocations equipped as evangelistic lay-preachers. Cliff does not exist to make ministers as such; it is a training school for evangelists.

III

ALL FOR EVANGELISM

ALL eager to reach my destination, I took no particular notice of the superb Peakland views on the road from Grindleford to Cliff. Frank Buckingham, a Devon farmer who was students chairman in those days, welcomed me. But I had arrived hours early ; so he introduced me to Ernest, a student who had been in the College one term.

It was Ernest who initiated me into the glorious tradition, and first told me the story of Cliff. He began with his own testimony. He said he knew more about that than anything else. " I was never any good at Church History and that kind of thing," he lamented. He spoke truth. It is reported that he was once asked in an examination what he knew about Erasmus. The answer seemed easy—" Wasn't he the man who invented shaving soap ? " But Ernest was a saved man.

He never knew his parents, and was reared in heathen darkness by distant relatives of his mother. In evil long he took delight ; then, one Sunday night, in a great industrial town, a fervent soul button-holed Ernest and took him to a Methodist Mission, where he was converted. He was immediately in trouble with his relatives. They cast him adrift for his religious convictions and he wandered for some months alone, longing for fellowship and counsel. Just then he met Norman Dunning, who was conducting evangelistic campaigns in the villages around Barrow-in-Furness, in co-operation with a fiery band of young local preachers.

It was in association with these revivalists that Ernest began his first public work for God. After a year's preparation he " received a note to preach among the Methodists " ; and Norman Dunning took him to his first appointment. He little realised that that service was the beginning of a new career.

He applied for entrance to Cliff, and was among the first company of students when the College re-opened after the Great War. It seemed ridiculous then to hope for entrance

21

into the ministry, and Ernest set his heart on returning to work in the shipyard. But, through the influence of Cliff, the impossible happened. After two years of evangelistic work, Ernest entered our ministry, and has since done wonderful work for the Kingdom of Christ.

After the testimony the story began. How he and I rejoiced that these magnificent buildings and this extensive estate were dedicated to the training of unprivileged youths like ourselves in the glorious ministry of evangelism. . . .

During the early months of 1850, the following notice, written in legal copper-plate, was displayed in the round bay-windows of the shops and inns of old-world Bakewell :

" Very desirable Investment in a Valuable Freehold Property situated in one of the most beautiful parts of the County of Derby.

" By Morris and Goodier at the house of Mrs. Greaves, the Rutland Arms Inn, in Bakewell, on Wednesday, 21st August next, at four o'clock in the afternoon (unless previously disposed of by private contract, of which due notice will be given).

" An Estate in the County of Derby, most delightfully and pleasantly situated, called Cliff House, and comprising a substantial and well-built Family Mansion of stone, and about 21 acres of excellent land, which surround the house in the form of a ring fence. . . .

" Cliff House is 33 miles from Derby, 9 from Chesterfield, 13 from Sheffield, Buxton and Matlock, 5 from Bakewell, and 34 from Manchester, to any of which towns the roads are direct, and kept in excellent travelling condition.

" To gentlemen having families, and desirous of spending the whole or part of their time in the country, Cliff House forms one of the most eligible residences in the country. The air is pure, remarkably dry, and calculated for health ; and the scenery is beautifully romantic and diversified. A range of lofty rocks, forming the boundary of the extensive east moors, is situated about a mile and a half on the east and serves to shelter the house from the north-east winds. The river Derwent is seen winding its course through the valley on the western side, and is overhung by a rich and extensive wood on the rising hill. The front of the house has a southern aspect which is very extensive, having the beautiful grounds of

Chatsworth with a view of the ducal palace from the upper rooms.

"A coach from Manchester to Nottingham and Newark passes immediately at the foot of the hill on which the house stands, and from Bakewell opportunities of travelling to almost all parts of the kingdom are afforded by London, Manchester and other coaches."

Cliff House was disposed of by private treaty to Mr. J. H. Hulme, the Recorder of Salford, who lived in it for some years after his retirement from office.

Mr. Hulme was a man of fervent evangelical faith and he had visions of Cliff House being used as a training-home for lay-evangelists. He spent some years preparing the estate for this purpose, but died before his hopes were realized. Nevertheless, he stipulated in his will that the place must be used "for the training of preachers, teachers, missionaries, or workers in any department of Christian service at home or abroad."

After Mr. Hulme's death, the house stood vacant for some time. Finally, in 1875, it was loaned to Dr. Guinness as a training-home for workers in the Regions Beyond Mission. It was here that Dr. Guinness conducted his astronomical research and wrote that once famous book, " The Approaching End of the Age "; it was here also that he and his great-hearted wife trained scores of able and devoted missionaries of the Cross.

They offered, without fee, a thorough training in Biblical and literary subjects to all unprivileged young men who wished to give their lives to the service of the Gospel; and there were special courses in languages, missionary method, and elementary medicine, for those who were called to service overseas. It would have gladdened the heart of the old Recorder to see Cliff House being used as Dr. and Mrs. Guinness used it.

No applicant was ever refused admittance because he was poor, but there were certain other rigorous conditions. Was he willing to co-operate by daily labour in meeting the costs of the training-home ? It ran by naked faith and the willing service of the members of the household. There were no endowments; and the candidate, therefore, might be involved in hardship.

Several extracts from a Guinness diary of those days bring

home that possibility. For instance, this : " Money matters may be, must be, a means of grace to those who have no banker but their Father in Heaven, and no great need of money but for their Master's work. We have found them so ! Is money wanted ? We must pray and there is little danger of formality in prayer when the payment of the butcher's and baker's bills depend on the answer coming speedily ! Does money come in ? We must praise ; for we realise so vividly His hand in its coming that our eyes are naturally turned heavenward with a heartfelt ' Thank God ' ere we take pen in hand to thank men. Is any expenditure suggested ? We must seek guidance from above ; for while, if we spend according to His will, He is sure to provide the funds, if we spend according to our own will, we may be left to our own resources, or lack of resources, and suffer accordingly."

Applicants for entrance to Cliff House had to be willing to suffer hardship, without any promise of reward or ultimate employment. They tested consecration by work and hazard in those days. Nor was this heroism the only test. I quote from the same diary : " Most especially we test the spiritual power of applicants by setting them to various forms of evangelistic labour. If they show real love for souls, if they succeed in turning many to righteousness, there can be little doubt they are calculated to be useful missionaries at home or abroad. But if, even though gracious and clever, they lack the evangelistic gift and spirit, nothing can compensate for the deficiency ; and they have evidently mistaken their vocation in aspiring to missionary service."

The conditions were spartan ; but, from the first day, Cliff House was packed to capacity with consecrated young servants of Christ. They were a most devoted company. The marks of their evangelical fervour are still all about the valley. The eastern boundary of the estate is craggy Curbar Edge with its " unhewn stones in random concourse hurled ". Upon many of those stones are still to be seen Gospel texts which were chiselled in by missionary students over sixty years ago. And there is a greater memorial of their devotion : before the nineteenth century closed, over fifty missionaries trained at Cliff House had given their lives for Christ on the Congo alone. They and their fellows had taken the Gospel to almost every unevangelised field, and many sealed the witness with their blood.

The Regions Beyond Mission used Cliff House for twenty-five years ; then, in 1901, the work was transferred to London.

Now the Trustees had to decide whether the property should still be used for the purpose to which it was dedicated by Mr. Hulme, or, according to a further provision of his will, be sold for the benefit of several specified missionary societies. They decided that it was no longer needed by any acceptable society as a training-home for evangelists ; and were awaiting a purchaser.

It was just at that time that the Joyful News Mission needed a new home. The work had outgrown the old quarters in Rochdale, and the first task of Champness' successor, Thomas Cook, was to find a bigger and better place.

We have already told how H. T. Smart discovered the place, and wired Thomas Cook. Together they went to view Cliff House. Behind the door of what is now the Common Room, Cook covenanted to do whatever God would have him do, if he would give him the place ; and God answered— " I will give it thee."

The process of purchase was beset by unforeseen difficulties, and at one time it seemed that Thomas Cook's desire might be frustrated. Others feared ; he simply rested in God's promise ; and the Trustees finally agreed to sell at a very moderate price. It only remained for the Charity Commissioners to approve the price and transfer ; and in faith Thomas Cook took possession.

The visit of the Commissioners' representative happened to fall upon a foul day of wind and weather, and the road from Grindleford station to Calver under such conditions is not a pleasant four miles to travel. When therefore he arrived at the College, despite a kindly welcome from Mrs. Cook—Mr. Cook was away from home—the representative was not altogether enamoured of the spot. After looking over the plans and asking several questions of Mrs. Cook, he faced round to her with, " Look here, Mrs. Cook, how much is your husband prepared to give for this place ? " " Well, sir, he is prepared to give £7,500, but no more, and the Trustees are willing to accept that amount." " Oh, very well then, leave it at that. It's all the wretched place is worth on such a day as this," he replied with a grim smile. " When is the next train back to Sheffield ? "

Thus did Cliff House pass into the hands of the Methodist Church. The name was changed to Cliff College ; and here, since 1904, the work which Champness founded has been continued and enlarged beyond all expectations, till now it is known and represented the world over.

The work grew apace under Thomas Cook's principalship ; and when the founder of The Joyful News Mission died in 1905, Cook proposed a Champness Memorial Wing, to double the capacity of the College. The Committee was reluctant. Wonderful things had been accomplished ; a sum of £13,000 was raised for the purchase and renovation of the property. They deemed it unwise to launch an extension scheme so soon. Cook felt guided, and covenanted that if God would give him a sign in the gift of £1,000 he would undertake personal responsibility for the cost.

A few days later, as he alighted from the train in Manchester, he met a friend who asked about the College. Was it full ? Had he any difficulty in getting students ? He replied that it was overcrowded and he was obliged to refuse scores of excellent candidates. " Why not enlarge it ? " said the friend. " Because I am waiting for the money," said Cook. There was a pause, then the friend said : " I have a thousand pounds of the Lord's money in the bank. I will give it to you."

In a few months the new wing was completed, and on the opening day, William Walker of Whitehaven put a slip of paper into the offertory box, bearing the words : " I.O.U. whatever you need at the end of the day." Thus God justified His servant's faith and the extension was opened free of debt.

Cook next transformed the old chapel in the lane into a simple but beautiful sanctuary. Then, when Samuel Chadwick was invited to become Biblical Tutor, a delightful house was built for him, on the hill, overlooking the College.

Immediately after Thomas Cook's untimely passing, Samuel Chadwick, who had succeeded to the Principalship, built the Cook Memorial Wing, including store-rooms, offices, and a well-equipped sanatorium. Students can be ill luxuriously at Cliff ! The southern windows of our sanatorium command the loveliest view we have of the beautiful Derwent Valley.

And since Ernest first " showed me over ", there have been greater and greater extensions. In order to conserve our privacy for practical purposes, it became necessary for Chadwick to purchase the two adjacent farms, and we became " landlords ". It became necessary also for us to have our own laundry and generating plant ; and the start of trekking necessitated accommodation for trek-carts and cycles. Then, in 1924, in response to the pressure of unprecedented requests for training, Chadwick built on to the old Champness Memorial Wing another block, comprising thirty bedrooms, domestic accommodation and a magnificent library, the opening of which was the occasion of the memorable visit of the Rt. Hon. and Dame Lloyd George.

One of Samuel Chadwick's dearest dreams was a little chapel to be built inside the College. The dream was not realised in his lifetime ; but it was built as a memorial of his magnificent life, by his friend and successor, the Rev. J. A. Broadbelt. It is a beautiful little Holy of Holies at the heart of the College life.

In addition to the new Chapel, within recent years, several workmen's cottages and a missionary rest-house have been built ; and the Guinness observatory has been transformed into a tutor's house. Now, at last, we have built a large Assembly Hall, with store-rooms, garages, and a caretaker's cottage ; for the accommodation of the Whitsuntide and Derwent Convention crowds.

When, just before his death, Thomas Champness visited Cliff, the contrast between the old place and the new evoked the remark, " I feel like a duck that's hatched a swan." What if he came to Cliff now !

The old manorial Cliff House can still be distinguished on its front side, but it is almost lost amid the modern extensions. The stabling and farm buildings were removed by Thomas Cook to make room for the Champness Wing ; and the old place, so transformed, is only a small part of a great institution, the extent and influence of which far exceed even the bravest dreams of the founder.

Now this tale of bricks and mortar would have little or no interest but for the fact that the upbuilding of Cliff has been a pageant of Providence. Every extension has its separate spiritual history—a story of God's glorious answer to faithful prayer for the provision of our needs. " Every bit of Cliff," Chadwick used to say, " represents some romance of Providence.   Every stick and stone and yard of ground has been prayed into our possession for the glory of God in the salvation of souls."

The prayer of faith alone created Cliff, and the same has sustained it.   That power of prayer was all that Champness had to rely upon.   He prayed in simple trust, believing that so long as the Lord meant the work to go on, the means would be provided, and that when they ceased it would be a sign that the Lord had other plans.   Once in mercy, as he afterwards saw, God tested his faith.   The income fell, and, in accordance with the covenant, he prepared to disband the evangelists. There were days of waiting ; then the ordinary happened. " Mr. —— says that as he was praying for us and our work, he thought he would send two hundred pounds.   We were praying.   I had asked all the men to pray before making an announcement in the paper."

It has been like that all through the story.   The work has lived by the prayer of faith.   Quarrier, the Müller of Scotland, used to pray with superbly confident trust, " We need seven hundred pounds this week to feed these bairns of Thine " ; and the manna failed not.   Nor has it ever failed in the life of Cliff.   Its story is a romance of prayer and Providence.

Cliff, therefore, as mere property, is a standing witness to the faithfulness of God.   But we rejoice in this estate for another reason, namely, that every yard of it, and everything on it, is dedicated to the single task that is dearest to the heart of God : the training of evangelists.   God gave it for this purpose, and more of it as demands and opportunities increased ; and we keep it for this purpose alone.   And one of our joys is, that by the terms of our deed, it will never be possible to use this place for any other purpose.   The founders believed, as we still believe, in the future of Cliff as a training-ground for evangelists ; and they dedicated it for ever to this task.

Already streams of grace have flowed from Cliff to the ends of the earth, and the best is yet to be.

IV

INAUGURAL

THE Inaugural Meeting on the first day at Cliff is still fresh in my mind. It did a lot to put my sense of inadequacy in abeyance to the spirit of hope. I began to believe in my own future.

The students were a motley crowd, drawn from all walks of life. The tutors were just as motley. I can see them now : Samuel Chadwick with his spare frame and leonine head ; Fiddian Moulton with his sturdy physique and the far-away stare of the traditional academic ; C. E. O. Rush, tall, strangely Christlike in facial features, and scholastic to the finger-tips ; Norman Dunning, youthful, slim, athletic, with a striking face in which there were mingled " a brilliant and romantic grace with trace on trace of passion, impudence and energy."

They spoke of the glorious traditions of Cliff in order to inspire us to worthiness and work. Fiddian Moulton was the first speaker. I recall the first effect of the curious falsetto in his voice. Moulton, like other members of his famous family, might have been a great academic, but the influence of the Moody and Sankey Mission in Cambridge changed the course of his ministry. Consciously thrilled then as always with his own part in " the College of the Unprivileged ", he spoke to us of the need for enlightenment in evangelism. Mr. Rush, to whom the memory of Thomas Cook was fresh and vivid, told us stories of his old chief's prayer triumphs, and urged us to work hard but pray harder. Dunning was autobiographical. We learned most of his story from the testimony of that morning—how he was converted and called to preach, how he was constrained to renounce a career in law for the sake of evangelism, the conversions he had seen in earlier days on the Yorkshire Coalfield and " only last Sunday night in Manchester "—all to stress the need for our consecration to evangelism.

Samuel Chadwick spoke last and longest ; and we listened with rapt attention. It was a great moment for me. He

29

described the beginnings of The Joyful News Mission. He
read Champness' charter : Our purpose is :—

1. To train evangelists, using the sons of Methodism, and
   especially poor and unprivileged youths, in evangelistic
   labours.
2. To be the ally and not the rival of existing evangelistic
   agencies.
3. To hold out no premium to unworthy motives, i.e. to
   offer no salary.
4. To secure none but efficient men, and oblige them to
   retire, if after a fair trial, they are not successful.
5. To send to the foreign field only those who have proved
   themselves equal to it by their work at home.
6. To pass into the ranks of the ministry those who have
   proved themselves fit for this work.
7. To depend upon the unsolicited gifts of God's people.

Having described Champness' great idea, Chadwick cited
Champness' saying, " Nothing pays like helping young
preachers," and urged us, on the authority of the long experience of Cliff with unlikely lads, to believe in her own future in
the will of God and the service of His Kingdom. He had
received a letter that morning from a man who came to Cliff
in 1907 from South Wales. He had had few educational
advantages, and had to begin the elements of grammar and
arithmetic after he was twenty-five. He was then too old to
be a candidate for the Methodist Ministry ; but he had a
passion for souls and the grace of determination. " He
entered the ministry of the Anglican Church," said Chadwick,
" took a divinity degree in the University of Wales, is now on
the way to a doctorate, and, best of all, is still an evangelist."

A story of that kind never failed to warm Chadwick's
sympathetic heart. From it—under spontaneous inspiration,
I believe—he went on to the story of his own beginning, with
slender resources and great disabilities, in public ministry.

" I had been at work from the age of eight, had been
handicapped with much sickness, and, as may be imagined,
my educational equipment was slender indeed. For years I
had struggled night after night with my books, and no one but
those who have passed through the experience can conceive the
difficulty of learning after ten hours' hard work. I toiled at
my task without help and without guide. Perhaps I accom-

plished more than I knew, but at any rate the discipline has given me great sympathy with the aspirations of young men who are trying to fit themselves for careers of usefulness. Theology I loved, but the mysteries of secular education were a weariness to a tired man. My sermons were my first concern, and they left me little leisure for other work. The Superintendent did not think me a suitable candidate, and told me so with brutal frankness. The offer of a lay agency came unsought, and I accepted it at the salary of £50 a year. At twenty-one I went to take charge of a large chapel in the Bacup Circuit.

"When I arrived on the spot I found a good Sunday School and a poor congregation. The problem was, how to get the thousands of people to Chapel who had no desire to come. In facing the problem I made the most important discoveries of my life. I learned the secret of power for life and service, and I do not know that I have added anything to the principles of successful work I found in those days of untrained and unordained service.

" No man could have been more inexperienced, but I found myself unconsciously led of God step by step. I began by allying myself with such forces as were to hand. It happened that the Men's Class was vacant, and I took charge of it. I was the youngest person in it, but it grew until we had to hold it in the Chapel, and had an attendance of seven hundred men every Sunday.

" I had a lot to learn in respect of my own limitations. My hope was largely in my sermons, but I soon found that eloquence and argument are lost on pews and pillars. When the little stock was exhausted the people were still outside. God searched me and cleansed me as by fire. There came into my soul a new sense of power. The Spirit of God came upon me. For seven years I had preached and seen no conversions. In twenty-four hours seven souls were led to the feet of Christ. The fire was kindled. Old feuds were healed, old sins confessed, old idols burned. Prayer meetings revived, and a passion for the lost took possession of our souls. A League of Intercession was formed and aggressive work organised. Every house was visited and an open-air campaign arranged. In all this I led and God graciously used me.

" My mind was led to the study of the raising of Lazarus,

and after I had expounded it at an early morning prayer meeting, earnest prayer was offered that God would give us a Lazarus. The prayer took possession of me. I could scarcely ask for anything else. I wanted God to give us a man whose conversion would strike the imagination of the town. And He did. On the hillside lived hundreds of quarrymen who were notoriously godless. One of them was notorious even in his notorious set for devilish and daring wickedness. We organised a Temperance campaign, which spread through the district. They made me President of Committee and Chairman of a great meeting held every Sunday night after the hours of worship. Thousands signed the pledge. One night this man donned the blue, and in a few days he was converted at our week-night service. Talk about a sensation ! No building was big enough to hold the people who came to see this man whom Jesus had raised from the dead. With his conversion there began the most wonderful revival I have every seen.

" I often look back to those days. In all my ministry I have done no better work, nor have I ever departed from the things the Spirit of God taught me there. The principles are simple. First and foremost a life fully surrendered to God and energised by His Spirit ; then hard work, much prayer, earnest study, no starch, plenty of sense, a passion to get souls to Jesus Christ ; and neither men nor devils can permanently hinder you from success in the Kingdom of God."

We sang one of Chadwick's favourite hymns :

> Lord in the strength of grace,
>   With a glad heart and free,
> Myself, my residue of days,
>   I consecrate to Thee.
>
> Thy ransomed servant, I
>   Restore to Thee Thy own ;
> And, from this moment, live or die
>   To serve my God alone.

Then we went out to the work—with his great words in our ears and hearts : " Believe in your own future in the will of God. . . . First and foremost, a life fully surrendered to God and energised by His Spirit ; then hard work, much prayer, earnest study, no starch, plenty of sense, a passion to get souls to Jesus Christ ; and neither men nor devils can permanently hinder you from success in the Kingdom of God."

for identifying himself with Bible characters, and entering very feelingly into " the historical situation."

One Friday night, we were having an examination on the Book of Habakkuk, the prophet of the watch-tower. Mr. Rush was acting as invigilator. Suddenly Crapper shattered the silence with a fervent Hallelujah !

" What is the matter, brother ? " enquired the invigilator.

" I'm up on the watch-tower with the prophet," cried Crapper.

" Well, you two had better be quiet up there till this examination is over," said Rush.

Chadwick was always at his best in The Clinic. It is probable that the majority of his students got more good from him there than from all his other work. We shared the precious issue of his own amazing ministries.

I treasure still the paper on which were written his final words on my own faltering effort. He objected to my speed, my Latinity, and my notes : " Cultivate leisure in preaching. Take time to put in windows. Take time to let the message sink in. Cultivate leisure in your style. Take time to be simple, lucid and Saxon. Never use a word of foreign origin when you can find one that is home-born. Take leisure to preach without notes. It will mean double the time in thinking, research, and soul-preparation, but it will increase your effectiveness many-fold. I would have you free from every hindrance that you may abound in power. The ease of mastery would save you from all kinds of bondage in phrase and delivery. When we preach, the Holy Spirit must have entire possession."

Now, let me not give a false impression. The work of the lecture-hall was very important. Through it, the Bible became a new Book to us, and we found new facility in preaching its message. But the altar, not the desk, was the vital centre of our life. After all, a man might know the Book, and have the gift of ready utterance, but if his own soul languishes within him, he is of no use as an evangelist. Cliff, therefore, keeps the altar-fire burning.

The devotional life is deliberately organized to foster Pentecostal Fellowship. The morning Quiet Time is guarded for private devotion. There are prayers morning and evening, and several prayer-meetings after dinner. We hold an old-fashioned Class-Meeting on Tuesday evenings, a service on Thursday evening, " The Joyful News Prayer Meeting " on Saturday evening, and services for villagers and students who are not out preaching on Sundays. And in the organized meetings a constant witness is made to the possibility of a triumphant Christian Life for every believer through the power of the indwelling Spirit.

Besides all this, there is the free devotional fellowship of the men ; and many old students associate the great spiritual crisis of their life with unofficial prayer-meetings on the moor, by the river, or in some quiet corner of the grounds. Here is a fragment from a recent letter written by one who was a student over thirty years ago : " Being at Cliff was like treading on holy ground. There was something about the place that encouraged men to pray. The whole place seemed to provide retreats for the quiet time. I remember one occasion when a number of us went to the observatory to hold a prayer-meeting. The atmosphere was alive. While Douglas Gray, now of Rhodesia, was praying, one was afraid to put out his hand, lest he touch God."

From the beginning it has been the custom for students to do two hours manual labour each day. The custom helps the College, but it helps the students more. In the earliest apologia for his methods, Thomas Cook wrote, " Every man who enters the College engages to take his share of manual labour, such as cleaning the other men's boots, waiting at table, cleaning the knives and windows, digging the garden and trimming the paths. This work is done of an afternoon, and besides being highly beneficial from a health point of view, prevents them from becoming snobs. One of the great dangers of raising a man from the coal-pit to a position of this kind is that he will lose his head. This system of manual labour, which even those who pay the full charge have to share, greatly diminishes the danger."

With two other brethren, one a surveyor and the other a miner, I was put to peeling potatoes each day for the whole community. I bear thankful witness to the supreme spiritual value of that fatigue. Fiddian Moulton used to say, " The tutors would be the very last to take offence at being told that the paramount educational influence of Cliff is that which is exerted by man upon man in the ultimate fellowship of daily corporate life." Well, that influence was always most free and active during " manual ". We talked and fraternized as we laboured ; and who shall calculate the mutual gain ?

Actual practice in evangelistic method is gained through weekly preaching appointments in the villages, week-end open-air work in the neighbouring towns, vacation missions, and summer treks ; and the mission-work is reckoned part of the training for every student. Men have the glorious privilege therein of equipping themselves for the larger service of Christ as they win needy souls into His Kingdom.

Imagine the gracious effect of a year's life in such a community upon men like me ! What did Cliff do for me ? Seven things :

1. It made me a student.
2. It gave me the clue to the Bible.
3. It put me on the trail of Pentecostal Religion.
4. It opened the door of the ministry to me.
5. It settled the character of my ministry.
6. It set me longing to help other unprivileged young preachers as I have been helped.
7. It made me believe in the validity of Champness' great idea : that the masses will be reached most easily and quickly by an order of evangelists raised from among themselves, an order of godly men able to speak their plain, straightforward, simple language, able to sympathize and fraternize with the common people, and win them for Christ.

VI

THE TRADITION COMES ALIVE

On the second Friday of my first term at Cliff we were visited by Captain Davis, the bookseller-evangelist, who was known to thousands on nothern market-places as a gallant soul and a great campaigner. Unschooled in letters, he was deeply learned in the things of God. Through the epochal influence of that visit to Cliff, I became intimately acquainted with him in later years. He was an extraordinary man, with the courage of a lion and the tenderness of a lamb. I once saw him tackle a heckling tipster round the middle, force him to his knees and make him pray on the open market-place. And by strangest contrast, he once made the most beautiful and trenchant (and perhaps the only) evangelistic appeal ever known in the chapel of Harrow School, and there were open decisions there also.

In early life Captain was a reckless sailor; but he had a praying mother. I seem to hear him now, telling that moving story of how he found a ship's cook, murdered in a drunken brawl, and how the shock helped towards the fulfilment of his godly mother's prayers. " I couldn't describe the scene I witnessed when I took his body home in a coffin, and as we followed him to his last resting-place.

" This awful tragedy did one thing for me—it made me hate the drink, and secretly I began to cry out for the living God. But for some time I argued : ' Yes, it's best to be religious, to have peace with God and rest of soul, to enjoy freedom from sin and to know one is right for heaven ! It is a great gift. But it isn't for me ; it is only for those who are born that way.'

" But oh ! ten thousand praises to God. I proved Satan to be a deceiver. I found Jesus did die for me, and that He could make me into a new creature. It happened while my vessel was in the Thames. I was led into Kenyon Baptist Chapel, and there I heard Mr. Leit Rozas, a Portuguese gentleman, preach, and after the service I got up and publicly confessed Christ. I crowned Jesus King, promising I would go where He wanted me to go, and do what He wanted me to do, and be what He wished me to be. And praise God, I found Jesus as Saviour as soon as I crowned Him King.

" My precious mother also prayed that I might become a preacher. Surely nothing seemed more unlikely ; but prayer alters things and makes ways where there are no ways, and things are brought to pass that otherwise could never be brought to pass. And now that I had found Christ, I wanted others to find Him, so next day I got my crew together in our little cabin and spoke to them about the Saviour. That was how I began to witness."

Very early in his Christian life, Captain wrote and asked Champness to take him for training in The Joyful News Home at Rochdale. The letter included evidence of the kind of consecration that charmed Champness ; so he replied : " Come as soon as you can, and stay as long as you like."

Champness discovered that sailors are not amenable to long schooling, and after one term he started Captain on his great career as a missioner. There were amazing scenes of converting grace in his services, especially in the open-air. He saw hundreds of conversions. No man of his own time had greater power for holding a crowd and winning converts on a market-place. And he had that power to the end. Only a few months before his passing, I saw the police move the over-flow of his audience from the tram-lines to safety, while thousands in the square watched his Gospel Cinema and heard his moving appeal for repentance.

His courage was amazing. Thomas Champness used to say, " I believe God has commissioned a special angel to stand by Captain, for I know no one so reckless." He visited all the public-houses and prayed in them at every opportunity. The inn-keepers appreciated this regard for their welfare and often invited him for meals. He was a happy warrior. Nothing affrighted him.

In the process of missioning through the years Captain gathered certain experiences and stories, some of terrible retribution and some of tender grace. I heard him tell them to the masses with his testimony scores of times, and never once without profound effect. He knew how to tell them, and he had the right voice for the job. On one fair-ground his powers of oratory were used to such good effect that the show-men had no chance against him. In desperation they sent a deputation to ask him to give them a chance.

Second only to his gift of pathos was his extraordinary faculty for laughing great lessons home to the hearts of the people. For instance, to support the point that unbelief is no use when calamity comes, he used to tell the story of an illiterate master-builder, who asked for a chance of witness from the mission-van platform, and spoke on this wise : " Friends, there are some folks who say there's neither God nor devil, heaven or hell. They say that when they are dead they'll be done for. Now I don't believe in this infiddlediddlety (infidelity). No, I don't believe in this infiddlediddlety. I am a builder and I once had a man who worked for me who talked like that. But he was working in an old house with me one day when the ceiling fell on him and buried him—and he began to shout, ' Lord save me, Lord save me ! ' I said, ' Can He 'ear tha' lad, can He 'ear tha' ? Ah thought there wasn't any God.' Friends, Ah tell thee, there's nowt like a rap on the napper for knocking infiddlediddlety out of a fellow."

When the Joyful News Mission was transferred to Cliff College, Thomas Cook invited Captain to take charge of one of his gospel caravans. A new caravan had been endowed, and a Norfolk farmer had given a horse, " the pick of nine," Mr. Cook used to say, " but remember, you never look a gift horse in the mouth." Old Duke cut some amazing capers.

The van was put into commission at Harrogate, and Captain went off in it with his young colleague, Robert Cleminson, who was himself a convert of one of Cook's first caravan missioners.

Robert Cleminson has scores of stories of those days of venture. There were hundreds of conversions ; and thousands of Christian books were sold to the people. He says, " The Captain was an amazing salesman as well as a great evangelist ; and he was a man of God. He spent hours in prayer and Bible-study each day. He was determined to redeem the days which wild living had devoured."

Once they had announced an open-air meeting in the market-place of a northern town. At the time of the meeting it looked as though they would have to abandon the idea. There were so few about. Then a man began to make his way across the market-place with most unsteady gait.   He was the worse for drink.   When he came near the van, the Captain's eyes sparkled.   The meeting would be held after all.   He jumped down and taking the man by his shoulders began to shake him violently.   And the man hollered loud and long. The hollering soon brought a mighty crowd.   Then Captain patted his unwilling helper on the shoulder, thanked him for getting an audience, and finally advised him to go home and sign the pledge. Captain spoke like an inspired man that night, and appealed for decisions. Fourteen souls accepted Christ. With what joy he related afterwards that four of those converts became local preachers.

He was tremendously keen to get the denizens of public-houses converted.   When he left one village, the policeman wrote to the sergeant in the next village, " Look after this chap. He gets all the drunkards converted.   We shall soon have nothing to do."

He prevailed upon a certain publican to let him hold a meeting in the tap-room on Saturday night.   Some of the customers signed the pledge and the publican's son went to the chapel next day and got converted.

During a mission in South Yorkshire he heard of a drunken blackguard who was reported to be the worst man in the town. Captain sought him out, and talked to him about the evils of drink and the power of Christ to save.   Trying to dodge the issue, the drunkard reckoned he had an appointment at a club. " Very well," said Captain, " I'll go with you to the club." He preached at the club and stuck to his man until he was converted.

Another of his exploits is best told in his own words : " I was at Hoyland Common, near Barnsley, with one of our old mission vans.   I had a service advertised one Sunday night at 7.30 p.m., but a drenching rain was coming down so that it was impossible to hold a service.   I went into the van and began to pray.   After a while I felt led to ask God to stop the rain. I was so certain he heard me that I got up from my knees and went out on the front of the van from which I used to preach. I saw a gentleman passing with umbrella and mackintosh, so I shouted : ' Stop, sir ! You shall see how much God loves your soul.   He will stop this rain and you will have a chance to get converted.'

" He was a complete stranger to me, but if I had searched the whole of England I could not have found a more sceptical man or one who loved more to laugh at Christians. I told him to put his umbrella down, and, to his astonishment, he looked up and saw the blue sky. He said, ' Why, this is strange ! ' and stopped to listen. When I made the appeal two men came into the van to give themselves to Christ. I closed the service, and while I was pointing these two men to Christ, I heard someone coming up the steps. Then the door opened and this gentleman fell on his knees and cried for mercy. He got gloriously saved. He was the postmaster, one of the best-known men in the district ; he lived a beautiful life and for the remaining twenty years of his life held many offices in our Methodist Church."

On the night of his visit to us Captain spoke on " Prayer in the Spirit." None who heard will ever forget it. He told us stories from the prayer-life of Finney, Müller and many others, but none so good as the stories from his own experience. He taught me more of the life of prayer in that hour than I had learned by all other means in the rest of my life, and I have not yet been able to improve on his Rules for the Quiet Time. But, above all else, he embodied before us, in his stories, in his record of venturous evangelism, in himself, the elements of the glorious tradition into which we had entered. Here, in vital form and ministry, was that utter consecration to the Lord for the evangelization of the masses about which Samuel Chadwick had spoken in the inaugural meeting. In living form it was an irresistible challenge and blessing.

Captain never knew all the good he did by that visit. That night many of us consecrated ourselves to the same task, and began our quest for the adequate grace and power. We had not long to wait.

VII

DAY OF EVANGELISM

THE old-time passion for souls never languishes at Cliff. The battle-prayer of the new generation of students is :—

> " Lord crucified, give me a heart like Thine,
> Teach me to love the dying souls of men ;
> And keep my heart in closest touch with Thee ;
> And give me love, pure Calvary love,
> To bring the lost to Thee,"

But every generation has a prayer like that, and every generation has maintained the same willingness to be led of the Spirit into any sort of enterprise to win the unconverted. Champness, always a pioneer, began the Gospel-car movement, and trained his evangelists to seize any means of saving men. Thomas Cook encouraged the same spirit, and kept a staff of sixty to a hundred evangelists who were ready for anything. He did not hesitate to disband the Gospel Cars, when it seemed that they no longer had their old appeal ; and he accepted eagerly any new prospect in effective appeal.

True evangelism is vital. The only unchanging elements in it are its essential message and purpose. Everything else is subject to adjustment. In method it accommodates itself to the thought-forms and habits of each generation, and aims to meet the need, suit the mind, and heal the heart of that generation. Otherwise, it fails. The evangelism at Cliff has always been vital and dynamic. It pioneers in soul-winning. Availed of a fresh anointing of the Spirit, the whole College suddenly embarks upon some new method of appeal, and another chapter is added to the glorious record. The forms change ; the old spirit of adventure and aggression abides.

We had such an anointing of the Spirit in my first term at Cliff. Many gracious influences prepared us for it : the general quickening of our spiritual life, the specific definition in all the preaching and teaching at Cliff of every believer's hope of constant triumph through the indwelling Spirit, Captain Davis' visit, and our knowledge that revival movements were beginning all over the land. There was much prayer for several days and nights ; then the Fire fell.

On the Tuesday evening of the first term we were gathered in the old chapel for our class-meeting.   Samuel Chadwick told us in greater detail the story of that baptism of the Spirit which changed the entire course of his life and ministry. He loved preaching, and went to his first work in Rossendale confident that good preaching would fill the empty church. It did not ; and, full of a sense of futility, he was flung upon God, who answered with fire, and made him an evangelist. He had not wanted to be an evangelist ; it was the farthest thing from his thoughts.   He knew he was called to the ministry, but he did not know what type of ministry.   But now great sinners began to come to Christ, and great crowds, unmoved by his earlier preaching, were lured into the Kingdom by the testimony of transformed harlots, publicans and criminals.   The crowd that would not come to see Jesus came to see Lazarus, whom He had raised from the dead ; and, seeing Lazarus, they believed in Jesus.

He told us that all he knew of evangelism he learned in the revival that followed his personal Pentecost, and that he had conducted his whole ministry by four discoveries then made— that the essentials of evangelistic power are sanctified personality, certitude of faith and a passion for God ; that conversions fill empty churches ; that our warfare must be carried into the devil's territory ; and that the spiritual church must be supplemented by a ministry of social sympathy. To that Pentecostal experience he traced all there had ever been of evangelistic triumph in his ministry ; and there had been much, as all the world knows.

After the Principal's address we went to prayer.   And that night Cliff experienced an outpouring of the Spirit unprecedented in its romantic history. To that assembled company there came a new vision of the redeeming Christ and the wide world's need. Many entered into an experience which lifted them into a new range of spiritual consciousness. Life henceforth thrilled with divine vitality. Assurance rose to certainty, duty was radiant with joy.   The all-pervading Presence brought a new sense of vocation and of power, and a new courage and a yearning compassion for Christless souls. The new spirit was fostered and guided to expression in a new venture of evangelism. This event was the beginning of the greatest era in the soul-stirring record of Cliff.

Norman Dunning became the leader of the new movement, and through succeeding years, he spent much more time outside the College than in it, leading its evangelistic campaign throughout the land.

The first efforts were small vacation missions, racecourse meetings and seaside campaigns. Our plant was primitive and our programme indefinite ; but we saw glorious triumphs of grace. Occasionally, we met hostility, as when Dunning and I were once threatened with martyrdom on Nottingham racecourse. Sometimes the authorities resisted our efforts. Once, we were refused permission to witness *on* the beach, so we chartered a rowing-boat and witnessed *to* the beach. Generally, however, we were well received. The people then had a mind to listen ; and we often had tremendous audiences. We preached for a verdict every time ; and there were some remarkable conversions.

On occasions there were amusing episodes. We were witnessing in the open-air at a seaside resort. A diminutive navvy, with a massive wife, came up to listen. Both were much the worse for drink.

In a little while the evangelist's challenge began to goad the navvy, and he was tempted to heckle.

" L . . . l . . . look 'ere, mister," he said, " thass all roight ; but can you tell uz weer Cain got his wife from ? "

" Tha' shut up," rasped the massive partner, " there be some folk wantin' t'know weer I got thee from."

But the navvy was not amenable to control. He repeated the question more aggressively.

" Well," replied the evangelist, " that question really doesn't trouble me. My problem is : where shall I get mine ? "

" Tha needn't let that trouble thee ; tha' can 'ave mine," retorted the navvy.

The crowd roared and the navvy was greatly encouraged. But he overdid it ; and some of the listeners, losing patience, asked him to be quiet. When he ignored the appeals, a young giant, very much the-man-of-the-world, walked over and faced him with a grim gesture.

" Who are you ? " enquired the navvy.

" I'm Bombardier Wells' sparring partner," replied the warrior, " and if you don't cut it, I'll . . ."

The navvy fled like a hare, and we finished the meeting in peace.

Later that evening, we held a meeting in a near-by church. Many of our outside hearers came to it.   The last speaker was making an appeal for people to come from their seats and kneel at the communion-rail, as a sign of their surrender to the Saviour.   There was no response, so the appeal was continued. By-and-by, the sparring partner, whose presence we had not noticed, came from a back seat and walked down the aisle. We thought he was coming to the communion-rail.   Instead, he stopped at the end of the aisle, half-turned to the congregation, and with the same menacing gesture said to the preacher, " Show me where you want 'em, sir ; I'll place the lot of 'em for you."

The sea-side work was developed with most gracious results.   There were some amazing trophies of grace.   I think of Percy Rush.

In his youth, Percy Rush knew saving grace, but he was a fugitive from God for many years during his middle life. He sinned himself almost insane.   I can only give excerpts from his story.

During his black days, he took a wild delight in the company of harlots.   Yet he occasionally found honour even in dishonour.

One woman of the town, Ada, a girl with raven-black hair and classical features, was the daughter of a minister in the North of England.   Because she had a child, her mother turned her out and her father was unable to prevent it.

" When I met her," says Rush, " she was, without my knowing it, dying of tuberculosis.   Her plight sobered me. I asked her if she ever prayed, and she, remembering her upbringing, scoffed bitterly.

" I believed then, as I know now, that you need be no plaster saint for God to use you.   More than once has God used a backslider for the conversion of some dying one, and He used me.

" At my suggestion, we prayed at the outcast girl's bedside, the prayer of childhood :

> " Gentle Jesus, meek and mild,
> Look upon a little child.

" She followed me brokenly. But when we came to the lines : ' In the Kingdom of Thy Grace, give a little child a place,' she said ' Give a sinful girl a place.'

" When we had finished she begged me to pray again, and I did so. What would some respectable Christians have said could they have peeped into that bedroom and seen the London prostitute and the backslider-profligate so engaged ?

" I never saw her again. But I heard. A few weeks afterwards a woman in black accosted me in a London public-house and begged half-a-crown for a wreath for Ada, who had just died.

" Presently, a tawny-haired Delilah came up and she too mentioned poor Ada. She had been the last person to see her alive. I called for drinks and she told me that before Ada died, she said : ' Try and find that lame fellow and tell him that I died praying that little prayer ? '

" The message hit me between the eyes. Declining Delilah's invitation to accompany her, I banged down my glass and rushed home."

Drink and drugs were his curse. He took them, he says, " to ease his human smart ", but they only increased the miseries of his hell on earth a hundred-fold.

Often he returned home like a fiend, to smash everything. Once a broken gas-bracket nearly turned the home into an inferno.

Meanwhile, his wife, convinced that her prayers would result in his cure, continued to pray and endure. Often he treated her brutally. Once a knife was broken as he tried to murder her.

On one occasion, after his wife and children had run out of the house for safety, he ran to his panel doctor shouting, " If you don't put me away I'm going home to do my wife in, and then I'll come back and do the same to you." They put him in a padded cell.

The Blessed Lord Jesus would never let him go ; and so he was always in torment.

" A civil war was raging within. I used to walk about the streets in utter desperation. Sometimes tears would stream down my cheeks. Once, as I was going up Ludgate Hill, a woman with a beautifully radiant face stopped, turned and asked me what was wrong. I told her. She said, ' God is dealing with you, and if you are truly penitent, He will very soon dry those tears.' ''

In a brighter period he went with his wife to Clacton ; and there they heard the Cliff students.

" We met some radiant, rollicking evangelists from Cliff College, where a cousin of mine was a tutor. During one of the addresses I jumped up and swore at the speaker. I was shouted down. A man behind rebuked me. I turned on him.

" ' Is this a place for sinners ? ' I demanded.

" ' For sinners,' he meekly agreed.

" ' Then shut up. This is the place for me ! ' ''

Next day his agony of soul was terrible beyond expression. As he walked along the Parade at Clacton, he noticed one of the Cliff speakers, and a voice within said : " Call him."

" No, no," said another voice, " see what a fool you will make of yourself ! ''

But he could no longer stand the strain. " Hi ! you," he shouted, " come here ! ''

They talked, and the penitent promised he would attend an open-air meeting that evening. There he stood at night, torn and harrowed by conviction, and the speaker was saying : " Who will stand with us beneath the blood-stained banner of the Cross ? ''

" Suddenly," says Brother Rush, " I saw a vision and I was part of it. A pair of strong supporting arms were about me. A voice like the murmur of many waters was consoling me. In the silence these words flashed into my mind : ' I have seen his ways and will heal him ; I will lead him also and restore comforts unto him and his. . . .'

" ' Is that for me, Lord ? ' I asked.

" ' Yes,' said the Mystic Voice.

" There was no white cloud in the blue sky above, but there was Something which only I could see—the thorn-crowned head and bleeding face of the Lord Jesus Christ.

" ' I died for thee,' said the Mystic Voice. ' When are you coming back ? '

" ' Now, Lord,' I said.

" Do not glibly tell me that this was an hallucination. I never expected such a vision nor desired it. It came to me, and similar visions are common in Christian history. Their truth and value can only be tested by results.

" And the result in my own life ?

" From that minute I was released from all my bonds. My diabolical hatred of my wife, of other people, my insatiable craving for drink and drugs, and even my desire for tobacco, were taken clean out of my life !

" That was ten years ago—and they have never once returned."

Shortly after his restoration, Percy came to Cliff to be trained as an evangelist. It was hard for him, so late in life, and in such a life ; but he took more grace and practical benefit out of it than any other man of his year. And ever since he has been preaching the Infinite Grace of Christ to other needy sinners.

Another result of that early anointing of the Spirit was a long series of evangelistic crusades in industrial centres. The supreme purpose was to win the unchurched multitudes. Accordingly, most of the work was conducted outside the churches. What triumphs of Christ's grace we saw ! . . . But that story has been told elsewhere.

VIII

WHAT MANNER OF MEN ?

WE are sometimes asked : What kinds of men come to Cliff ?
The answer is : All kinds.

Here are a representative few :—

Brother Will was a steady-going fellow, economically sure
and well satisfied with his life, who felt he had no need of faith.
But someone took him to the Linacre Mission and the preaching of H. M. Nield disturbed him.

As soon as he was converted, Will began his apprenticeship
in evangelism with the Mission Brass Band up and down the
streets of Bootle. Open-air work was still a thrilling job,
but Will wanted more—he felt he must preach.

Now, truth to tell, Will was not a brilliant brother. He
had a big heart, a burly figure and a boisterous voice, but not
a nimble brain. It took him six years to become a fully
accredited lay-preacher. It was not that the Local Preachers
Meeting doubted his call, and Will himself certainly had no
doubts, else discouragement had overcome determination
long before the end of that long discipline. It was simply
that Will's earlier way of life left him so far sort of the standard
set by Methodism for its local preachers.

At last he approved himself to the brethren, and was
" accepted on the Plan."   Then, in order to equip himself for
wider service, he gave up his work and came to Cliff—just
before the Great War.

How he worked ! Fiddian Moulton, for years afterwards,
used to cite Will's colossal efforts to learn, as a condemnation
and spur to laggards.

Half-way through his year he was elected College Chairman ;
and he was so good at it that he made history.

One of the great difficulties involved in re-opening after the
Great War was the fact that there would be no one to hand on
the tradition of the place, in respect of things which belong not
to the class-room so much as to the fellowship between the
men themselves. The Cliff tradition is one of prayer and
fellowship and enthusiasm, which cannot be taught, but only

communicated, and it seemed as though there was going to
be no one who, from among themselves, would be there to
act as medium between the old and new generations of
students. Under genuine inspiration, the Principal asked
the Leeds Mission to lend Will to act as guide, philosopher and
friend, to the new men. No one better could possibly have
been chosen. As pre-war chairman, Will had exercised a
powerful influence, exercised it in a manner which made
authority an inspiration. Although he was now a minister,
and very busy, he came. It was a great boon to have him
back ; and none can tell how much he did for the continuance
of the tradition.

And while we owe a debt to him, Will just as fervently
confesses his debt to Cliff. " It gave me a chance in life just
when I needed it most, and fitted me for the work to which I
was strongly convinced God had called me."

Throughout his ministry Will had been a missioner, and at
present he is exercising a remarkable ministry in Newcastle at
the Hall where Moody began his first British campaign and
Sankey's harmonium created a first-class sensation.

I quote now from a recent appreciation of his work published
in a northern daily newspaper : " This sturdy champion of the
Gospel may be seen on Wednesday nights during the summer
months in the Bigg Market, and frequently on a Sunday
morning on the Quay-side, handling crowds of many hundreds
of men of the hard-headed Northumbrian type. Not every
minister is qualified for this important kind of work, where
sometimes the influence of drink and the bitterness of fate act
as explosives on the motley audience, but, with that radiant
smile and iresistible good humour, he can quell the most
turbulent spirits.

" Nothing is finer than to hear the evangelist of Rye Hill
swaying a thousand men with the message of Goodwill, and
winning back some who had lost their way in the maelstrom
of this present world. Few preachers in the city could tell
more thrilling stories of the triumphs of his outdoor ministry
than this torch-bearer of the grand old Gospel."

.   .   .   .

Not all our men belong to the dispossessed and unprivileged
class.

Brother Charles is a son of the manse. To the influence of his home and the Christlike devotion of his Irish parents he owes a great debt.

At the age of seventeen, he left the boarding school and entered a large business house as an apprentice. He says, " I had no sense of vocation, and no particular interest in the tasks in which I was engaged. Outwardly I was, I imagine, a rather colourless youth, and inwardly I was suffering from a vague sense of futility, the direct result of a lack of Christian conviction."

Like most children brought up in vigorous evangelical traditions, he had made several early attempts at discipleship, and there is no doubt about the genuineness of these experiences ; but during the first months at business, though maintaining the outward forms, he completely lost the sense of reality in religion. Thus he faced the difficult period of later adolescence without a living experience of Christ ; and bitter were the strivings and humiliations of those years.

He sees now that God was at work in his life, and his sense of failure was really conviction of sin. " Thus it was that when—in November, 1921—I attended a series of evangelical services in my father's church, I was ready for repentance and a decisive Christian experience. After a sharp and bitter inner conflict, I yielded my life to Christ and publicly expressed my new allegiance to Him."

Through the years there have been other spiritual crises, vivid experiences of consecration and renewal, but that surrender in 1921 was the turning-point of his life.

One result of his conversion was an immediate conviction that he must give his life to missionary service. He did not see how that was to come about. His school record made him modest about his own mental capacity, but he now had, for the first time in his life, a real hunger for learning, and he determined to find some means of satisfying it by disciplined study. He began to read his father's books, but the experience with them revealed his need of consecutive training.

At that time, Charles knew little or nothing of Cliff College. But *Joyful News* came regularly into their home. In its pages he gleaned a certain amount of information about the College, and, without consulting his parents or anyone else, he wrote one day to the Principal, the late Samuel Chadwick. To his astonishment Chadwick invited him to go to Cliff.   So, in the autumn of 1922, he left Ireland for the first time—acutely conscious of his own limitations, but terribly in earnest, and eager to learn—and made his way to Cliff.

At Cliff, Charles made great gain.   The fellowship of the brethren was an incalculable blessing to him.   He is a reserved brother, and the deeply religious life of some of the brethren sometimes found expression in an ebullient fervour to which he was not accustomed ; but Charles found gain in it all.

His letters are full of gratitude for the influence of every member of the staff ; but it was Chadwick who influenced him most : " All Chadwick's teaching and exposition were suffused with the passion of an ardent evangelist, and they quickened within me the burning desire to win men for Christ."

Perhaps no man of his year took more good from Cliff than Charles.   He was not even a local preacher when he entered the College ; but almost immediately after his return he entered the Irish Methodist Ministry and, after further training, was sent to India as a missionary.

The evangelistic, social, and educational ministry which Charles exercised for several years among high-caste Hindus is one of the epics of modern Methodist Missions ; and now he is doing an equally wonderful work among " The Untouchables." Cliff rejoices in his triumphs for Christ, and is thankful to have had some part in his training for the glorious work in India.

" The year at Cliff," he says, " resulted in a remarkable quickening of my spiritual and mental life.   My experience there fired me with two ideals which have largely helped to determine the course of my life and ministry : (*a*) the desire to be an evangelist, and (*b*) the conviction that true evangelism must be based upon hard and systematic study.   These ideals, vaguely present in my thought before I went to Cliff, really came alive there under the stimulus of inspiring teaching and concrete opportunities to put them into practice.   As I seek to do the work to which God has called me in this land, I frequently recall with affectionate gratitude the fellowship at Cliff, and give thanks for all that it has meant to me in the discharge of my supreme task."

.   .   .   .   ?   .

Though it would be impossible to reproduce it, we shall never forget the Firebrand's first testimony at Cliff. It was so naïve, so frank and fearless, so full of wonder at the grace of Christ. Again and again he lapsed into dialect, and when we laughed at it he said : " We'll get t'understand wun another sum day."

He told us of his wild youth. At twelve years of age, he was in trouble with the police for stealing pork pies. A little later he started Sunday School, but " T'vicar turned me aht for bein' 'opeless an' unmanageable." He went to work in the pit, and grew up at once. " Ahm sorry to say," he went on, " t'influence of t'chaps I worked wi' didn't improve me behaviour. I were just a swearin', thievin' pit lad, up t'all kinds of devilry."

Some one persuaded him, with his gang of pals, to join a new troop of scouts. One of the troop rules—the most impossible of all—was that its members were to attend some place of worship. They went, full of fun and foolery, to Kexbro' Methodist Church for several Sunday evenings. Slowly the influence of grace began to prevail ; and then, on one never-to-be-forgotten Sunday evening—" March sixteen, nineteen-nineteen, at a quarter t'eight, when Bill Challenger, t'bishop o' Kexbro', were appealing "—our friend walked out to the penitent-form, followed by his pals ; and kneeling there, he became a new creature in Christ.

The news of his conversion spread quickly. " ' Wot ? 'Im ? ' they said. ' Ah well, tha' knows it'll no' be for long. ' E'll never stick it.' The check-weighman said : ' If tha' sticks it till Christmas I'll buy thee a 'ard hat.' I got t' 'at all right, for at Christmas I wuz a Local Preacher on Trial."

At this point he went off into a most humorous description of his first attempt to conduct public worship. He was helping another lay-preacher, and was to " oppen t'service." He was very nervous, and after giving out the number of the first hymn, he said to the congregation : " If any o' you wants t'feel queer, come up 'ere."

He began to speak in the open-air, and was soon entrusted with a little service by himself. That night several souls openly confessed their acceptance of Christ as Saviour ; and that experience made him an evangelist for ever—" An' now Ah've cum 'ere, t'learn 'ow to do it better."

Not at once, he told us, did he possess all his possessions in

Christ. There was a controversy with the Spirit about
certain idols. One by one they were surrendered—" But I
stuck to me pipe to t'bitter end." One night, in a prayer
meeting, this struggle about the tobacco habit reached the
climax. A great conflict went on in his soul while the friends
sang :—

> " I surrender all . . .
> I surrender all . . .
> All to Jesus I surrender,
> I surrender all . . ."

" At last," he said, " I got up an' went forward to claim
deliverance, an' all t'way to t'penitent-form I were singing '—

> " I surrender pipe-an'-bacca-an'-all,
> I surrender pipe-an'-bacca-an'-all,
> ALL to Jesus I surrender,
> I surrender ALL."

Now it may seem pifflin' to you, but it was a Waterloo to my
soul, and when it wuz won, I wuz free. 'E 'ad all o' me, an'
'E's 'ad all o' me ever since."

He worked in an open-air mission band, distributed tracts
from door to door, and " came on trial as a local preacher."
He loved the evangelical witness and travelled miles to hear
evangelists ; and he secretly cherished the hope that some day
he too might be sent to evangelize the masses.

Someone introduced him to *Joyful News*, in which he read
about the work of Cliff for unprivileged youths who feel called
to preach. It was that information which encouraged him to
think that even he might one day conquer his illiteracy and
be made fit to preach the Grace of Our Lord Jesus Christ to
needy men in a wider sphere.

James Barlow heard his testimony in the Square at Keswick,
and sent him to Cliff for training, in the hope that his longing
to win souls might be realized. Then began the struggle with
illiteracy.

It was impossible to make the Firebrand all he wished to
be ; he was so far back at the beginning. We have often
heard him tell a crowd, " For most of one term I couldn't
understand the words. For instance, somebody told me the
next lecture was about homiletics. I'd never heerd t'word
afore. So I went and looked into t'diction-airy, an' all I

could find was 'omelette—a fritter of eggs,' an' I thowt I were in for a lecture on cookery, though I couldna' tell wot use that were to a preacher."

He loyally bears witness to the patience of the staff and the love of the brethren ; but really it was a joy to help him, even though improvement was slow.   He struggled with his studies, " Trying," as he says, " to be my best for God."   In view of his beginnings, we thought he had done quite well in the College ; but, with all our faith, not one of us expected that he would ever be able to do what he has done for the Kingdom of Christ.   We knew that he was on fire for God, and all felt the tonic influence of his rollicking devotion ; but no one imagined that he had it in him to become so powerful an evangelist.

I remember being very impressed by an entry in Wesley's Journal : " God sends by whom He will send . . . I read prayers, and Mr. Whitfield preached.   How wise is God in giving different talents to different preachers.   Even the little improprieties both of his language and manner were a means of profiting many who would not have been touched by a more correct discourse, or a more calm and regular manner of speaking."   As Whitfield was used, in spite of, nay, because of his deficiencies, so has the Firebrand been used—amazingly used, all over this land, to win a host for Christ who would never have been touched by " a more calm and regular manner of speaking."

IX

THROUGH CLIFF TO THE MINISTRY

A THIRD of the men who pass through Cliff return home, to do better work as lay-preachers among their own folk, a result in which we greatly rejoice, for Champness' chief aim in founding the work was to supply evangelistic local preachers. One of these brethren is doing a magnificent work in a needy town in County Durham among his neighbours and friends. He has led fourteen relatives to the Lord Jesus Christ; and has organized a Mission Band to take the Gospel message to all the villages around.

Another third of our men serve under various evangelistic and social agencies at home or abroad; and the remainder enter the ministry of various churches, but mainly of the Methodist Church.

Among the last-named there are scores of men who owe their position entirely to Cliff; and their stories are full of romantic interest.

.   .   .   .

Brother Reg was the son of a prosperous business man who took to drink and lost everything. The business was closed down, the home sold out; and Reg's mother died of worry.

The family was scattered, and Reg went to poor relatives. He became a morning newsboy with a branch of W. H. Smith and Sons; and for five years rose at 5 a.m. to meet the news train. After six months an evening round was added, and his wages rose to four shillings. On his thirteenth birthday he left school and became a full-time newsboy at eight shillings a week.

For several years he did odd jobs in London. Then he went to South Wales, and found better employment in a chemist's warehouse. It was there that Reg found his way into the service of Christ.

With memories of boyhood days stirring within him, he

joined the Methodist Church. A stranger in the town, with no friends, he was glad to do it. The chapel-keeper—once an outrageous character but converted in a common lodging-house—befriended him. He threw open his little cottage to Reg by night. He drew him into a slum Sunday School where he became a teacher. He led him to join a lodging-house Mission Band. He took him to class. He built up his spiritual life ; and when the call came, he coached him as a local preacher.

These were five happy years, in spite of the hardship he still had to endure. Souls were saved in his services. He was accepted by the common people ; and he began to study hard in the hope of entering the ministry.

"It was a forlorn sort of hope," says Reg. "My lack of education made me fearful, and my fear was deepened when my minister felt that he could not yet nominate me as a candidate for the ministry. Great was my disappointment. It almost broke my heart. Then came a surprise. My class-leader offered to send me to Cliff at his expense. I felt this was divine leading and was full of gratitude for this opportunity to improve myself. I was so conscious of my need of education, especially in literary subjects, that I was ready to go through any toil at Cliff to get it."

At Cliff, Reg was in his element, with a chance to study the Bible under guidance, to learn the art of sermonising, and to tackle grammar, arithmetic, history and English literature free from distraction. But richer blessings than these were in store for him. "I began to discover what it is to sit in heavenly places with Jesus Christ. What grace came upon us ! What power took hold of us ! What joy filled our hearts ! "

Not a moment did Reg waste at Cliff. It was hard going for one who was not a scholar. Although Bible-study was a delight, literary subjects were a continual grind. As a candidate for the ministry he had to put in extra hours of study. Often he was up at 4.30 a.m. Cleaning boots at 6 a.m. meant exemption from manual labour in the afternoons, allowing additional time for study : so he cleaned boots every morning. He did his utmost and succeeded.

"Since those days," he says, "I have looked back frequently and wondered just what Cliff did for me. Cliff did more for me than I can tell, for every time I think, some new debt occurs to me. Chiefly, I thank God that it decided the course of my ministry : it made me an evangelist for ever."

. . . .

Happy, too, is a Cockney. He was born in the London Maternity Hospital, City Road. His coming had been dreaded by his mother. All her other children had died in infancy, possibly through malnutrition or some other plague of that Shoreditch slum. Would she keep this one, or would he go the way of the others ? Well, she kept him ; but really it was a miracle that he survived.

Landlords were afraid to collect their rents in the district where Happy lived. There was a pub at every corner, and the sad issue of drunkenness in almost every home. It was an area in which publicans, pawnbrokers, bookmakers and flinty-faced money-lenders thrived. Happy's people suffered under the whole hierarchy.

Happy's home was eventually spoiled and smashed by strong drink and when he was eight years old, his mother died through sheer neglect. Immediately after the funeral his father deserted the family, and Happy was taken to the work-house with his sister.

Eventually the poor law officers found the father and then began the frequent " flittings " with the change of foster mothers. Living in this London borough, then moving into another London borough, from being under the charge of one woman to another—poor bairns ! Yes, sometimes as a boy he thought about God, wondered if there were boots or shoes in heaven ? But his religious thoughts never softened him. Let anyone touch his sister and he could use " 'is mitts ". Same if anyone laid a finger on Happy ! Those two motherless bairns fought for each other like tigers.

Time came when Happy had to fend for himself. Kicked out of house at fifteen, he began to mix with the " Men ", and in Nile Street, Hoxton Street, and Whitecross Street he " learned things." Life became more of a tragedy to him, for in those streets there is little of the beautiful, apart from the brave women who fight adversity. The pubs, run by wealthy brewers, are haunts of corruption and degradation.

In a healthy reaction, Happy joined a training-ship ; and

" bein' a kid wot noo 'ow to use 'is mitts," he took up boxing ; and he really had a chance of becoming famous. But just at that juncture, Lucy Heel of the Leysian Mission got hold of him, and held him till he was converted to the Lord Christ.

Then back he went to his old haunts in Nile Street ; but now to lead open-air meetings. " You men know who I am, what I was, but now, with God's help, I mean to finish with the old ways. Jesus is precious to me, and I want Him to be precious to you."

The Superintendent of the Leysian Mission at that time was Rev. J. Ash Parsons, a saint beloved by all, and he saw that arrangements were made to send Happy to Cliff College.

Would we had space to record Happy's days at Cliff. He says, humbly and gratefully : " Cliff made me."

Now he is doing magnificent work for God as an ordained minister in Methodist Missions.

.   .   .   .

Arnold has made a brave stand for Christ. He belonged to the Scout Troop attached to the South Kirkby Mission ; and had won a scholarship at Hemsworth Grammar School. Best of all, he openly yielded his life to Christ one Sunday night in the Mission. He wanted to be a real Christian ; but it was hard going, for he lived in a queer home.

Arnold's people were poor. His father was the leader of the local Communists. Through working as an agitator in the pit, he was victimised, and was for a long time out of work. But he always found money for drink. Very often on Saturday evenings, about closing-time, you might have seen Arnold furtively looking down the road for his father. For, though the grace was all on one side, Arnold and his father were great pals.

After a while, Arnold's sister was converted. Then Pastor Belcher suggested that Arnold should begin to pray for the conversion of his father also. There was a wistful look on his face ; Arnold thought it was hardly possible.

In July, 1934, Hugh Redwood visited the Mission. On the previous Saturday night, Arnold's father had been felled outside his own drinking club, with the result that on this very day, with two lovely black eyes, he was lying on an old couch in the kitchen, sucking away at his pipe. Hugh Redwood and Belcher visited him. Both talked to him about his soul, about his boy, about his influence in the village, about the Christ who could revolutionize the world if he and his comrades would obey His commands ; but it seemed all to no purpose.

" I am going to pray," said Hugh Redwood, " the Pastor and I are going to kneel down by this couch and ask God to do what we can't," to which Jim replied : " I'm not stopping you." Hugh Redwood suggested he might take the pipe out of his mouth, to which he replied : " I don't see why I should." Hugh Redwood asked him, " If Jesus Christ came in at that door wouldn't you show him some respect ? " to which he replied he might, but Jesus Christ wasn't coming in anyhow.

Hugh Redwood asked God to do what he couldn't, to reveal the Saviour's grace to this needy brother. Then the visitors left.

Some months later, at a Prayer Meeting preceding special services, Stanley Belcher told the people " Next month, Arnold's father will give his heart to God."

On Sunday, February 24th, the Rev. R. J. Day, preaching in the Mission, made an appeal, and the first one to respond was Arnold's father. He soon became a helper in the Sunday School, the Guild and the Men's Meeting. In a few weeks, his wife, Arnold's mother, knelt at the communion-rail seeking the Saviour—also in answer to the lad's prayers ; and to-day six relatives are members of the Mission, all won through Arnold's prayers.

Now Arnold worked harder than ever at school, and matriculated. When that was done, he got his heart's desire, permission to apply for admittance to Cliff.

He came to Cliff in October, 1936. " I had wanted to come," he writes, " ever since I had my first taste of their fellowship when a Trek came to South Kirkby. Because I was originally going to be a teacher, I had remained at school longer than usual, always attempting to convince my parents that I was called to preach the Gospel. When my father was converted and my whole family affected by the powerful influence of the Lord Jesus Christ, there was no objection to my obeying God's call. I immediately asked if I could go to Cliff ; and Cliff opened its doors to me."

Cliff did a lot for Arnold. I quote his own record : " It

opened the eyes of my spiritual understanding. My life was challenged by its gracious influence, and, as never before, I became really and truly surrendered to God. He opened the windows of heaven and blessed my soul. Cliff taught me the cost of prayer and made me realize its power. The Bible became a new Book to me. I came to realize more and more the need for evangelism. After Cliff I spent a year in a circuit as a lay pastor and the experience I gained at Cliff stood me in good stead. Cliff made me realize that a passion for souls is vitally necessary to every preacher of the Gospel ; and I have lived and shall live my ministry for Christ in the power of it."

Arnold was finally accepted into the Methodist ministry and is now training in one of our Theological Colleges.

.   .   .   .

Scores of other instances come to my mind.

I think of the little fellow from East Anglia, who was ordained two years ago. He was one of the first to seek my help after I returned to Cliff as tutor.

When I asked him on his ordination day what Cliff had done for him, he hesitated—" Not for fear of saying too much," he explained, " but for fear that I might under-estimate my debt."

As I watched his studious face I recalled his humble beginnings with us. He was a shy, reserved, quiet little disciple of Jesus from a poor home. He worked hard to master the elements of English, and did very well at it ; but we were all surprised when he gained acceptance to the ministry. Since then, however, he has gloriously proved his call.

He was ready to answer—" Well, one thing can be stated clearly—I should never have been in the ministry but for the help you all gave me in ' the College of the Unprivileged ! ' My mother made great sacrifices that I might spend a year within its fellowship and it was during that year that I felt called to the ministry of the Methodist Church. In a private conversation which I was privileged to have with the Principal, before I left Cliff, I voiced my keen desire ' to do the work of an evangelist '. His rejoinder was that there was no better opportunity for such service than that afforded by the Methodist ministry, and I have since proved the truth of his words. . . . It was at Cliff that I felt that challenge to aggressive evangelism which I regard as the ministry's principal justification and responsibility."

Then we fell to talking about his wonderful work in the East End of London. I remarked that while he sympathised with social service, it seemed that he was still, in his chief allegiance, a wholehearted evangelist. He replied : " Through my short experience of East End life and conditions I am convinced that the only message which can give ' new lives for old ' is the Gospel made familiar to me, and efficacious for me, by Cliff. Cliff did many things for me—things which have been tremendous value to me in my work, but the one thing for which I shall always be grateful, is that I learned there, through that intimate knowledge of the Word of God which Cliff gives—that I was sent to declare God's eternal purpose— the reconciliation of men to Himself and to each other in Christ Jesus."

I would like to trace out for you the heart-moving story of how that little evangelist found both himself and his mission in the College of the Unprivileged. And I would like to tell the story of John, a Liverpool Street arab who came to us. He was shockingly illiterate ; and he had no thought of entering the ministry, till he discovered that God had given him power at Cliff to prevail with sinners. He entered the· Methodist ministry in 1930.

One of Cliff's chief glories is that it has put scores of poor boys into the ministry who otherwise could never have attained it.

X

CLIFF OVERSEAS

THERE are Cliff men everywhere. Before me as I write are messages from all over the world.

Here, for instance, is a letter with a photograph of fourteen former Cliff students, who are now ministers in connection with the Methodist Conference in Western Australia. For the first time in the history of that Conference, a Cliff man occupied the Presidential chair and the brethren foregathered to signalize the occasion.

Here are brotherly epistles from Fred Cottrell, Sam Pollard's successor among the mysterious Miao, W. A. Beckett in Dominica, Douglas Gray in Rhodesia, Brother Copperwheat in Paris, Fred Chapman on the Ivory Coast and several others —all thankfully remembering the gracious influence of Cliff.

From Berar, Gordon Price and C. F. Moss, new recruits from Cliff to The Kirku and Central India Hill Mission, report their first reactions to the dire need : " A visit to the Hindu quarter of the city revealed to us strange gods and strange customs—

> " From god to god they rove,
> And many gods abound,
> But yet they have not found
> The One True God of Love."

We wished many times that we could speak their language and tell them at once of the love of Jesus for them."

There is another Cliff man at work in the same area, under another mission. While he was with us as Cliff, he gave no promise of outstanding missionary power. His background was very poor ; and, truth to tell, we felt that we could not encourage his desire to go to India. But he went ; and in the first month he led ten Anglo-Indians to Christ.

There is many a romance hid in the missionary annals of Cliff.

As a youth Bennie Mackay followed the sea ; and he soon forgot the influences of his godly Scottish home. His mother

64

was a saintly Salvationist with her heart open to every breeze of revival.

When revival broke out on the north-east coast of Scotland, just after the Great War, his mother took him to the meetings, and he was well-nigh converted. They were gracious days. " How well I remember those meetings," writes Bennie. " There were no messages, a hymn, prayer poured forth, and souls were crying for mercy. This was true of every church in the village, and souls were saved everywhere, in the streets, at sea, and often in the night a seeking sinner hurried to some saint's home to find the Lord. Such were some of the experiences of my childhood ; but I did not let the Spirit use them to my salvation."

After training he was sent on a tramp-steamer to South America. That first voyage was his undoing. Only two of the crew were decent ; the rest were a drunken blaspheming lot. At first he was horrified at their doings ; but soon he joined in.

He wandered far in sin, but he was always restrained from the grosser kinds by thoughts of his mother, till she went suddenly to Heaven ; and then. . . .

But it was not to last long. Bennie's brother was converted on a battleship in the Mediterranean ; and the Spirit of God was working in other ways. But Bennie shall tell his own story.

" Early in 1932, I was in Shanghai on the deck of a cargo steamer with all its bustle and noise, clattering winches and shouting coolies, and there I came face to face with God. My whole life came before me, its emptiness, the futility of my efforts and ambitions, and I realised I was a sinner. Almost the very next day a letter arrived from my brother in Malta, telling me in detail of his conversion ; it was then I realised that Christ was the only way to new life and forgiveness.

" Then followed six months of terrible soul agony and despair, until I arrived home ill.

" While I was at home ill, the new Methodist minister came. He had been at Cliff. Before entering the ministry he had worked in the pits, and knew how to preach the Gospel to the common people. The Chapel filled. I went to hear him.

" They gave me a seat against the pulpit. The preacher had persuasive ways. The text was Job xiv, 14 ; and the message was for me.   Then came the appeal.   I was trembling from head to foot, my heart going like a steam hammer.   God was speaking, and during the appeal I rose to my feet before all my own people, looked into the preacher's eyes and said " I will ".   When I sat down a great peace filled my soul. I knew Jesus was mine.   I had the witness of the Spirit.

" Such a thing had not occurred for some time, and the whole place knew of my conversion before Monday morning. Soon afterwards, I went fishing for two months, to get enough money to help me study for my Second Mate's Certificate.   At the end of 1933 I passed the examination, but was far from satisfied.   God was calling me out."

Eventually Bennie came to Cliff.   Here he received his call to the mission-field and the Fulness of the Spirit to make him adequate for its demands ; and now he is doing fine service for the Gospel in a desperate area of the Sudan.

Brother Dan Smith is another Cliff-trained missionary. Now he is exercising a remarkable ministry among tribes of Miao, Tisu, Lolo, Korpu and Tai in the far-east corner of Yunnan.

His own account of the spiritual preparation for his great work is best : " I found salvation in a Methodist class-meeting to which a ship-yard work-mate invited me.   Mr. Fountain led the meeting.   That man's face glowed with the joy of inward religion.   His message seemed aflame.   I shall never forget it.   Two things happened in that class-meeting. The Holy Spirit gave me a knowledge of myself and exposed my inward need as a sinner lost and undone, and at the same time gave me a realising view of Christ as my Saviour.   I knew that he had died for *me*.   There in Him I saw comfort for my soul, a refuge from wrath, balm for all my wounds, and grace to save.   There and then He saved me : I knew He had made me a child of God.

" My early Christian life was marred by self-will.   I needed more instruction in conformity to the will of God, and more discernment in the fear of the Lord.   But alas ! 'that daughter of pride, enthusiasm,' often led me into folly.   My service was in the zeal of the flesh, not the power of the Spirit.   I needed the wisdom from above, likeness to Christ, more knowledge of the Scriptures, and deeper communion with the Spirit.   It was this need that took me to Cliff.

" The fellowship of Cliff is the greatest force for God that has ever come into my life. I was one of an inner circle. The four of us enjoyed many a solemn hour in the Holy of Holies. Our rooms often became 'the gate of heaven'. We prayed and studied together. The enlargement of our Redeemer's Kingdom was all our desire. Cliff sent us forth to be evangelists. In team campaigns and trek crusades we learned to disregard both the applause and rage of men and speak as Elijah did to Ahab—'I stand before the Lord God of Israel.' As students we were taught the value of souls and the need of warmly urging hearers of the Word to embrace Christ immediately. Many a blessed praise meeting we had on Sunday evenings in our student days, and in later days as evangelists, as we offered to God the fruits of His increase.

" It was in the early days at Cliff that God finally dealt with my corrupt heart and life, after I had been seeking inward holiness for months. For three days the Spirit plunged me into darkness. Conviction was deep and intense. The thing which polluted my life, poisoned the springs of it, and brought me sometimes under its power, appalled me ; and I hated my sin as never before. The devil sang my praises, to keep me from doing the right, but the Holy Spirit intensified the conviction until I rose in the presence of all my brethren to publicly acknowledge my need. The Spirit gave me the word ; ' The God of peace sanctify you wholly, body, soul and spirit ; faithful is He that called you who also will do it ' (I Thess. v, 23). And just then He did it. My soul was filled with perfect love to Christ, and the Holy Ghost bore strong and powerful testimony that His sanctifying work was done.

" My call to China also came at Cliff. The reading of Hudson Taylor's biography impressed me. A visit from Miss Mildred Cable convinced me ; and here I am now, witnessing for Christ in a strange land, during times of desperate need.

" Of my own work I would rather not write. Immature missionaries are not the wisest recorders of mission work. Yet I praise the Lord because my few years of labour have not altogether been in vain. I was designated to a lonely station in Yunnan. These high mountainous regions are the home of many aboriginal tribes. They are most affectionate people, and our work among them is joyous and blessed. There have been solemn seasons when the Lord came down and visited His people."

Quite the most remarkable part of Dan Smith's work is the effect upon missionaries and native evangelists of his burning witness to Sanctification through Faith in the Power of the Indwelling Christ. I quote from a recent report in *China's Millions*.

" Brother Dan Smith made the greatest impression on the students, and, as a result, chiefly in his meetings, but also in our meetings as well, many came out for confession of sin and to seek regeneration. One result of the Bible School was that two of the students with the pastor, Chang Chih Ch'eng, went on a revival campaign to the Nosu out-stations. During the past six weeks they have seen over four hundred people at the penitent-form, confessing their sin, many of them in tears. Among the number have been one or two elders and several deacons, as well as some eighty people who came to the Lord for the first time."

In addition to the scores of Cliff men who are labouring among native races, there are scores of others at work among the English-speaking nations. Before me as I write are letters from all over the British Empire ; and in a letter from the far West, Brother C. H. Brown says that he has met Cliff men at work in almost every corner of the United States.

And that reminds me of Brother Brown's own story, with which I shall close this chapter.

He was not always a globe-trotting evangelist. He had been in business for some years when God called him to evangelistic work. He gave up the business and came to Cliff. At Cliff he found his life-work and the ampler grace needed to carry it through.

After several years of itinerant evangelism, he undertook to become lay-pastor of a derelict church in Leeds ; and there carried through a most remarkable transformation.

The Ventnor Street Church had seen great Gospel triumphs in earlier times. But now it was closed. Around was a population of thousands of people untouched by organised religion. The congregation had dwindled to a handful, the collections were insufficient to meet expenses and the Church was closed. It had been closed for three years. The windows were broken ; the place was derelict.

Several industrial concerns offered to buy the premises, but certain leaders in Methodism who saw the possibilities of the place, refused permission. But they needed a man of vision, faith and grace to re-open it.

By a series of providences, Brother Brown was singled out as the man for the venture and he consented.

The first step was to renovate the premises, and a sum of nearly £500 was subscribed by direct giving for the purpose. A few weeks later, the Church was opened with great rejoicing, and in the opening service five people were converted. Then the amazing story began.

By the preaching of the Word alone, with emphasis upon Scriptural Holiness as the vital condition of effective evangelism, a new and glorious church was created in less than a year.

When the Methodist leaders who had been at the opening services returned to the first anniversary, they heard it reported that the Sunday School was full, and they had a large and efficient staff of teachers—all converted. They had started a Class Meeting on Tuesday nights, and the attendance week by week had been about one hundred and fifty people. Sunday by Sunday the congregations had increased until now the church was full every Sunday night. Best of all, there had not been one week during the year without conversions, and among the converts were people of every walk of life, who, as soon as they were saved, were marshalled into the soul-saving mission of the Church as active workers.

What was the secret ? Just prayer and insistence upon the evangelistic vocation of believers—the Cliff conception of a soul-winning Church. There were no bazaars, no stunts, and no social provisions ; but five prayer-meetings a week, straightforward Gospel preaching, and ceaseless evangelistic enterprise. "We go for souls every time," replied Brother Brown, when I asked him for the secret, "We go for souls every time and all the time, and we have never had a barren week."

XI

THE College maintains a permanent evangelistic staff composed of men who have taken its training, and have, in the process, shown the practical signs of evangelistic vocation. These men conduct seventeen-days campaigns throughout the winter, and generally lead the students in their vacation campaigns.

They do amazing work and achieve amazing results often under the most adverse conditions in needy churches.

Every week they send reports of their work to the College. From these I shall extract a few representative stories.

. . . .

The following report tells something of the effect of two missions, a year apart, which one of our evangelists conducted at Outwell, near Wisbech.

" We are sometimes asked ' What happens to the converts after your missions ? ' There is a great answer in this place. Just a year ago a number of young people were converted. They formed themselves into a mission band, and through winter and summer they evangelized most of the villages in this circuit. They have had the joy of leading over thirty people to Christ by their testimony. Moreover, their witness has created a fervent desire for evangelism among the members of the circuit and district, with the result that six missions have been conducted by Cliff evangelists in the neighbourhood.

" A second mission-band has been formed at the extreme end of the circuit and is doing a similar work. The Outwell mission-band has already sent two young men to Cliff to be trained as evangelists, and now two other young men are very anxious to come to the College.

" My first week-end was just like a continuation of the mission thirteen months ago ; and, indeed, as one of the officials said, the interval has been a continual mission. The church is ready and willing for any kind of evangelistic adventure. For instance, last Friday night I abandoned the

ordinary service and went with a band of young converts to
'mission' the nearest public-house. We had a mixed recep-
tion, and there was a certain reserve among the clientele.

"I offered to play the champion dart player, and it seemed
that God blessed the darts. We won their favour. Then we
sang and witnessed. In a little while we were called to the
'select room', from which we had been previously banned.
There also we sang and witnessed to the power of the Gospel.
We were requested to come again and we returned the next
night. Before we left, twenty men were reading the *Joyful
News*, which they had bought, and we made friends who
might, as we prayed, be won for God before the end of this
mission.

"In addition, this has been a season of refreshing for
believers. They needed an anointing of the Holy One ; and
at the end of one service, twenty-three people came seeking
the answer of grace. Most of them were just over a year old
in the Faith. This also has resulted in real effectiveness in our
work for Christ."

.   .   .   .

God gave Champness a special concern for village Methodism. It is still with us ; and in its power our evangelists
devote themselves to needy village causes with wonderful
effect.

Here, for instance, is the story of a village cause which had
become small and disheartened. Brother Clayton was sent for
a mission. Young people were converted, including five of one
family, who formed themselves into a mission-band which not
only rejuvenated the home church, but evangelized the
district, and revived several neighbouring congregations. They
have won many souls for Christ.

The following report is typical : "On arrival here I discovered that no Sunday School had been held for many years,
and only five aged members comprised the Society. From the
first meeting when only two gathered, the attendance has
gradually increased. Last night's crowd of twenty was a
record ; and we were blessed as a local preacher and business
man realized the claims of Christ and fully surrendered his life.
For seven years this society has struggled on with an attendance
never exceeding ten ; yet I believe the doors have been kept

open for these days of special effort. This church will live and thrive."

And here is the story of a village Pentecost : " On Sunday night over fifty people came out to the communion-rail, some seeking salvation, others seeking the indwelling of the Holy Spirit. Testimonies were then given freely, while sinners wept under the burden of their sins. The Spirit of God was present in marvellous power. On Monday night we were again blessed. We had our biggest crowd and at the close of the meeting an old local preacher openly confessed his luke-warmness, and prayed for a passion for souls. Others sought the Saviour. We pray that the fire will spread to the surrounding district."

One of our evangelists conducted a mission in a little Suffolk village. God blessed him to the entire neighbourhood. One day, during visitation, a mother and daughter asked him the way of salvation, and he led them both to Christ. One night three women walked several miles to get converted in his service. In a popular meeting late on Saturday night, he pointed two men to the Saviour ; and one of them said with shame that he ought to have yielded to Christ several months earlier when the Trekkers visited his district.

" It has been a glorious mission," wrote the evangelist. " In all there have been twenty-one conversions. Yet I feel as the disciples felt when Jesus told them to rejoice rather that their names were written in Heaven. What He condescends to do through me is glorious ; but best of all is what He did *for* me—

> " Precious, precious Blood of Jesus,
>   Shed on Calvary ;
>   Shed for rebels, shed for sinners,
>   Shed for me."

Another evangelist conducted a campaign in the Methodist Church at Halmerend. Here is his closing report : " On Sunday and Monday the rail was crowded with seekers—a fitting finish to a great mission. The secret of the success lies in the fact that these people know how to pray. Many nights fifty people have gathered for prayer, interceding on behalf of the Gospel service to follow. Over one hundred decisions have been registered. Christians have been filled with the Spirit, and sinners converted to God. Such scenes as these have never before been witnessed in this church.   This is the Lord's doing and it is marvellous in our eyes."

.   .   .   .

There are several outstanding stories in this year's record, of which the following is one : " The holding of a Cliff College Mission in February, 1938, marked the beginning of a new series of activities and blessings at Stanfield Church.   The evangelist came to a church which had many opportunities for aggressive work.   During the mission there were many converts, most of them young people.   On the three Sunday nights, open-air meetings were held in High Lane, the favourite Sunday parade of hundreds of young people from a wide area.   The opportunity was taken of inviting them to an eight o'clock rally in the church.   The result was surprising. Young people belonging to our church—some of them new converts—stood outside and asked people to come inside.   The church was filled, and on the last Sunday night the communion-rail was too small for the number of people seeking salvation most of whom were in the church for the first time.   After the mission, the ' Sunday Night at Eight ' services were continued.

" To improve the occasion, it was suggested that much good work could be done by holding a tent campaign in the summer. A team of men were sent from Cliff, and then the Trekkers came.   The Campaign proved a blessing to many.   Work was continued by way of personal invitations on High Lane, and many outsiders were reached.

" One of the men brought to God by this means was a man who would never have attended a meeting inside a church.

" This is his story : As a young man he taught in a Sunday School, but through trouble in his home, he became embittered, and made vows that altered the whole course of his life.   One day, thirty years ago, he threw his Bible at the vicar, and never entered a church again.

" Ultimately, he became an advocate of atheistic Communism.   Then came the Great War, and his life in the army was one of continual rebellion against authority.   He incited the troops to disobedience.   He was court-martialled and did penance for blasphemy.

" After the Great War he became leader of an Atheistic Society, and did much harm to the cause of Christ.

" This kind of life went on, until one night, when walking along High Lane, he met a fellow-Communist who pointed out to him the ' Tent ', and mockingly suggested that if he stood by the fence and pretended he was watching the cricket-match in the next field, one of the young people would ask him to the meeting inside. This he did and was duly invited. He replied that he was an atheist, but being pressed to come, he promised to attend.

" True to his promise he came. Several young people marked him out for special prayer, and sought to win him for Christ. On the Friday night it was found that he had not come to the Tent Meeting. Two of the young people went to his home and brought him along. That night he made an open confession of his conversion, which had taken place that morning, in a remarkable way. At noon—was it when the Cliff men were holding their usual prayer-meeting ?—he swore at a man, and was about to do so again when some restraining power held him back. Immediately, there came to his mind the text, ' Come, let us reason together.' At once he knew that there was a God, and the reality of that moment is still with him. After the meeting he asked God for forgiveness and prayed that he might be made as aggressive for the work of Christ as he had been against **it.**

" On the following Sunday night, he gave a powerful testimony to the direct working of God in his heart. The Almighty used his testimony that night to the conversion of many more. His friends were cynical and told him he was too intelligent for this experience to last long ; but he is still with us and bears an effective witness. The change that has come over his very countenance is sufficient testimony to the truth of the Gospel.

" Since the Tent Campaign the work has gone on. A Young People's Fellowship has been started, the Sunday evening service has improved, and the whole spirit and tone of the church is different. Most of our members look upon it now as a means of aggressive evangelism among the outsiders. The ' Sunday Night at Eight ' meeting has been held for the past year ; and during the winter months, from among those who have been brought in from outside, about sixty young people have come out to the communion-rail, to signify their surrender to Christ. Many of these belonged to other churches as children and have joined up with them again, and are doing active work. There is a vigorous life among the people of the church. They found an experience of Christ during the Cliff Mission, and they have ' a mind to work ' for the furtherance of His Kingdom."

.   .   .   .

Among those who listened to the Trekkers at Bridlington last August were two local preachers. They were members of a church which was then in a very low spiritual state, and their own spiritual condition was not above the average. The radiance of the Trekkers shamed them, convicted them and made them enquire into the promise of Pentecost.

Filled with the Spirit, they returned home resolved to change the history of their church. Much prayer was offered and finally the leader of the Bridlington Campaign was sent to conduct a mission in their church.

It was a remarkable mission, and there were scenes such as had not been witnessed in living memory. Eighty people openly sought the Saviour ; and that church was re-born.

Among the converts was a notorious drunkard. His wife could not remember a night in their married life when he came home sober. He made the home a little hell. But it is all changed now. We teach our evangelists to go for the worst ; and this man was held until he was saved. Two nights afterwards his wife also was saved. They are now members of a mission-band which regularly witnesses outside the public-house which the husband used to frequent ; and already the converted drunkard has led several old friends to Christ.

Revival fire is spreading from that church to other churches, and already a town's evangelistic campaign has been suggested.

So we go on, seeking by all means to win the people for Christ, according to our ordination as a mission to the masses.

XII

EVANGELICAL TROUBADOURS

EVERY summer, our students, as a vital part of their training and in fidelity to our charter, trek through some part of England, preaching Christ to the common people. We have sent out such treks every summer since 1924.

It all began in a vision that came to the late Samuel Chadwick while he was lying very ill. He saw afresh the great spiritual needs of the masses, and he saw that Cliff had to make a new attempt towards meeting those needs.

" The vision as I see it," said Mr. Chadwick, " is to send forth a band of young men, Cliff-trained, full of faith and the Holy Ghost, to preach Christ to the multitudes unreached and unsought by the Churches. They will receive no salary. They will go as they are led, and they will live by faith. They will take no collections, solicit no subscriptions, beg no favours, but tramp from place to place, preaching and singing in lanes and streets and market places, depending on God for every-thing, and sleeping anywhere, like the Friars of old. We do not know what developments may come."

The movement began as soon as the vision was known. A party of ten young evangelists set out on trek, blending the joyous devotion of Francis with the world-embracing passion of Wesley, and making glorious history. They tramped nearly five hundred miles. Where the Church was willing to co-operate, it was made the base of operations, but the appeal was always to the outsider. All the way they preached and testified, and everywhere they saw men and women converted.

Each year in increasing numbers, but in the same simple way, the Cliff Trekkers have taken the road, singing their choruses and telling their story of saving grace. In parties of eight or ten, they have trekked thousands of miles. They have borne witness on village greens, and market squares, on crowded pleasure beaches, and race-courses, to crowds of every size and kind. Everywhere they have found a ready response to their appeal. Men and women living apart from God and His

Church and with " no use for religion," have been arrested by their message, and savingly converted. On the other hand, young people brought up in Christian homes and nurtured in religion have felt the pull of their real and joyous message, and been led to confess Christ, and so to find a personal experience of Him.

Here is a typical story, written several months after the events which it describes :

" The coming of the Trekkers was an unusual episode for Brighouse, and their visit was like a breeze from the hills of God. I had arranged with the Corporation for the best open-air stand in the town. We kept to the same place, at the same time each evening, with the result that, whilst we had a good crowd for the first meeting, it grew larger each night.

" Interest was maintained, but there was no visible result until the last evening, and then just as we commenced the meeting rain began. The Salvation Army Hall was near, so while our open-air meeting was in progress, I went and asked the officer in charge if we might come in, as I feared the rain might disperse our crowd and souls be lost. Permission was immediately given—so we asked the crowd if they would go to the Army Hall. They agreed, and we marched in procession singing Gospel songs.

" Soon the Hall was filled to overflowing. Several of the Trekkers testified and Brother Clayton, the leader, made the appeal. One after another stood up, as a token of surrender to Jesus, till fifteen were on their feet, and they stood for some time. The meeting closed, and then the brethren dealt with the seekers individually, till they all ' got through.' I took their names, and the churches with which they proposed to ally themselves, and then I passed the names to the ministers. To the best of my knowledge all these seekers are standing firm to-day. In fact, one church official told me to-day that the two young people who joined his church were not only standing, but were bringing others in.

" I am hoping we shall be able to have another party of Trekkers this summer, and for a week-end too. Send a lot like the last. The homes in which they stayed still feel their influence. They were a grand lot, every one of them—a splendid proof of what Christ can make of fully-surrendered lives. I was proud to be associated with them, and more proud of the place which they represented. With renewed thanks—God bless you all.

Sincerely yours,
J. W. B."

And here is a beautiful letter written by a lady to a young Christian.

Liverpool,
26–7–38.

" My dear M——,

" I was so glad to hear that you are still standing fast. Don't mind your friend regarding you as a Christian. However unworthy you feel, she is quite right. All who follow Christ are immediately born into His family and have the unspeakable honour of calling themselves by His name. That is why we must be so very careful how we live—so as not to dishonour the Sacred Name.

" I must tell you of a very happy and wonderful experience we have had here lately. Every summer the students of Cliff College (a training centre for evangelists) go ' on trek,' eight or ten groups of them, with a hand-cart containing the very simplest equipment.   They tramp from place to place, preaching the Word, just like the first disciples of Jesus—having no money, but trusting God to provide for their needs. They stay for a few days in this centre or that, sleeping on schoolroom floors, holding meetings, indoors and out, preaching no particular sect, but simply inviting everyone to come to Jesus.

" Well, one team came to Liverpool, and their first halt was at Admiral Street Mission. My word ! what a tremendous lot of good they have done—especially in my own soul. They have made me see the abject poverty of my spiritual life, and called me to a deeper consecration and closer walk with God. I am willing that He should use me now in whatever sphere He may need me.

" During the past month, they have visited five churches in the city, of different denominations, and a marvellous succession of conversions has followed their witness. We shall not know the full result until we reach ' the Other Side.' I thank God from my heart for the faithfulness of their ministry. They were young men, eight of them, drawn from all walks of life, as different temperamentally as could well be imagined, but utterly one in their love of Christ and absolutely ablaze for Him.

" Many of us who loved the Lord before, have had the dull embers of our spiritual devotion kindled to a flame. Best of all, many others who walked in darkness and the shadow of death, have seen a great Light. I must tell you of one of them.

" Edith, a girl of eighteen, came to the open-air meeting in a mocking mood. The trek-leader spoke under guidance of Christ's dealing with the woman who was taken in adultery ; and he made the Saviour's words thrill with life—' Neither do I condemn thee ; go and sin no more,' and I was asked to talk to her.

" She told me one of the worst stories I have ever heard. She was living with a married man, who is separated from his wife—a filthy story. But she had heard the appeal of Christ and wanted to give Him her heart. We went to the chapel and prayed with her. She left that place a changed girl.

" Pray for Edith. She works in a very poor class café, where she is already witnessing to the power of Jesus to forgive and change sinners.

" God bless you M——, and may you grow to love Him more and more. There's no turning back, now—is there ?

" With loving thoughts and prayers,

Yours always,
" E ".

.   .   .   .

Before me as I write are many letters full of gratitude for the ministry of the trekkers—one from a West Riding vicar, several members of whose flock found Christ on the village green ; one from a young man who was converted during a visit of the Trekkers to the live little church at Norton ; another from a farmer, whose boy yielded to Christ in a market-place through the witness of our students. And here is the testimony of a man, who was saved last Leger Day at Doncaster.

Cliff men have preached at Doncaster Races as at several other race-meetings, every year since 1920 ; and some of our greatest trophies have been won there.

Last Leger night, our men took their stand among the tipsters and cheap-jacks on the market-place as usual. Early in the meeting a smart young man came up to listen. He was born in a Christian home, and had Church associations in his youth ; but he lost his soul through business prosperity. In recent years, most of his gain and time had been spent in clubs, hotels and bottle-parties. Then suddenly the flow of money stopped, and he found himself out of a post. On Leger Night he was on the way north to get help from his father's friends.

As he had to wait for a train he took a walk through the market-place, and came at last to where the Trekkers were witnessing to a big crowd. He says " I felt very lonely and ashamed as I listened, and I began to think of the wasted years. I compared myself with those young fellows on that platform. When I could bear it no longer I walked away, to see what else the market had to offer. By a power which I now know to be the power of God, I was drawn back again to the Trekkers. As one after another got up to tell what Jesus meant to him, I kept wishing that I hadn't made such a mess of my life. At last, an old school-friend—Luther Porter—stood on the platform, and as he began to tell how the living Christ had influenced him, in his business, in his daily life, I began to yearn for the same Saviour. It was evidential pleading. I saw that no man in his own strength could or would stand on the market-place in his own town, to testify before people who know him, with the chance of being scoffed at, unless Christ was more real and vital to him than anything else in the world."

When the appeal was made he grabbed a decision card, and darted out of the crowd, afraid of breaking down ; but two of the Trekkers followed him ; and that night, he says, " I gave what was left of a broken life to Jesus, to be used by Him as He wills."

> " 'Tis worth living for this ;
> To administer bliss
> And salvation in Jesus' Name."

XIII

SALVATION AT THE SEASIDE

EVERY summer since 1920, we have sent evangelistic teams to the most popular seaside resorts. As a mission to the masses, we follow the multitude every time.

During the first week of the campaign at Bridlington last August, we paid the team a surprise visit.

When we arrived the meeting had just started, and the crowd was small. The people were difficult to draw at first, but the brawny leader knew what to do. There was in the team a little man who was a well-known comedian till a year ago. The leader put him up, and in ten minutes his music-hall technique had drawn a tremendous crowd. There must have been two thousand hearers on the four terraces.

When the crowd had gathered, the converted comedian offered to get down. " No," said the leader, " give them your testimony."

The little man mentioned his name and many people in the crowd knew his history. He told them he was not always wayward. In early youth he loved the sacramental worship of the Anglican Church which his godly mother attended, but his life on the stage quickly led him into the ways of transgression. Yet he never quite lost his love of beauty, truth and goodness. The conflict within him made him most unhappy, and he longed for peace. Someone introduced him to Miss Martin of Bradford, and after a most miserable tour, he talked things out with her, and gave his life and soul to Christ.

He did not leave the stage immediately, and actually his work did not hinder his life in Christ, but at last the Spirit led him out. " Whereas I thought it my mission to witness in the profession, I soon learnt that I had to give it up in order to preach the gospel. Then God guided me to Cliff. This is a wonderful new chapter in my life. I cannot express all the joy of it. At every checking-up I see how Jesus has shown Himself to me in some different way, some new beauty has drawn me closer to Him, some new gift of power sends me singing and laughing through the grounds, or some new glimpse of just what the Cross means sends me silently to my knees. I have found Him the everlasting secret of peace, power and satisfying service."

A member of the team who had just been accepted into the Methodist Ministry played a piano-accordion—and we sang a famous hymn to a music-hall tune. The leader gave out each verse with sound Gospel exposition, and the crowd joined in the singing heartily. It was a clever way of making an unwilling crowd hear a sermon on saving grace. Then the man with the best voice recited the Twenty-third Psalm and a few well-known Scripture passages which were deliberately chosen to evoke childhood memories.

In a moment's pause at the end of the hymn, a youth on the second terrace informed us that religion is the " opium of the people." The leader responded by calling up a man, who, for several years was a Communist agitator. This was his testimony : " I know the people as well as anyone, and I have suffered in their cause. The cause of the common people is still very much in my thoughts, and I still hope for a social revolution, only since I came to Christ, I have seen the utter necessity of a prior moral revolution.

" I was converted in May, 1937, at the age of twenty-seven, after leading a life that was useless and empty. The Lord Jesus found me in a country lane in Kent and took me just as I was, absolutely ignorant of spiritual matters, steeped in sin, and with a heart full of hatred.

" I have never been under parental control or known any form of discipline since leaving school. At the age of fourteen I was acquainted with all the vices possible. Later my vagrant desires led me about the land, and I often slept out.

" I became interested in politics, studied Marx, and was soon helping to wage ' the class struggle ' in the ranks of the Communist Party. I was away from home, in Birmingham, living in the headquarters of the Communist Party.

" In 1934 I went on the National Hunger March from Lancashire to London, two hundred and thirty miles. Whilst in London I was ejected from the House of Commons.

" I had no time for religion, for I regarded it simply as a powerful instrument of the Capitalist System. Parsons and policemen I hated. I ridiculed the Church and thought all that was necessary was a sound economic system, where everyone had material security.   Then there would be no need of prating parsons, the Bible or Jesus Christ.

" Despite my vehement hostility, Christ found me.   I was working as an ice-cream vendor, and I suddenly became conscious of His Presence.   All against my will I was brought into contact with a parson, who evidently loved me as a soul for whom Christ died ; and I liked him.   Just before I left home to work in Kent, he asked me if I was ready to accept Christ, but I refused.   I was afraid of the consequences and the risk to my reputation.

' I thought that my new mood was just some queer emotional strain.   I told myself that when I went away, it would wear off, and then once again I would renew my hostility. Somehow or other I could not escape the feeling, and when Jesus Himself challenged me I could resist no longer.

" It happened in a country lane in Kent. When I reached my lodgings that night, I went upstairs, and got on my knees by my bedside, and there I asked Christ to forgive me, a sinner. I soon felt that inexplicable peace steal into my whole being, and ever after I was, and still am, eager to testify openly to Christ.

" I went to Cliff in September, 1937, shockingly ignorant of the Bible.   But I did know the saving grace of Christ, and I have gone on faithfully with Him.

" Now here I am, witnessing to you, a new man in Christ, with one supreme desire : that you should know Him too, and find in Him, the only real hope of this war-ridden world."

That testimony had tremendous effect and Brother Butler called me up to " put before the people the heart of the matter," that is, the fact that the essence of the Gospel is an offer of divine grace in Jesus Christ to redeem a man's life from sin and selfishness and recreate all his relationships in righteous love.   Then we appealed, and there on the open terraces, before a great crowd, several people openly confessed their surrender to Christ.

It was a remarkable meeting, typical of many others in that wonderful campaign.   One evening, during the third week, as twilight descended, a solemn hush came over the meeting, and hearts that a little while before had been careless of the things of God, were gripped with deep conviction. Surely it was Christ in the midst, as of old among the needy folk of Galilee.   He spoke the word of pardon, peace and power to fourteen seekers. Hallelujah !

. . . .

While such good work was being done at Bridlington, similar campaigns were in progress at Withernsea, Mablethorpe, Skegness, Yarmouth, Lowestoft, Morecambe, Blackpool, New Brighton and Douglas.

In every place there were glorious times of converting grace. The Blackpool leader sent in this report : " This is our fourteenth campaign at Blackpool. A local mission-band which was formed after our first campaign, stands with us every year ; and we have the loyal support of the ministers.

" Once again we have had the joy of seeing all sorts of people openly confessing their surrender to Christ. One man came with tears running down his face ; gripping my hand, he said : ' Coming here to this meeting has meant everything to me. I'd lost hope ; I'd given up everything religious, but to-night I have been restored.'

" After one meeting I was handed this letter :—

' Dear Brother,
' Owing to being at work, and not able to put in but little time in being present at your meetings on the sands, and having good faith in your evangelistic efforts of bringing people to the foot of the Cross of the Lord Jesus Christ, and praying most earnestly that the Spirit of the Lord shall be poured out on you all and those that shall hear the word of testimony, I give you a little to supply the needs of your mission.
' I remain, your brother in the Lord,
' ANONYMOUS '

" The writer of it had enclosed half his week's wages.
"At the closing rally, the communion rail in Adelaide Street Church was crowded with seekers. Souls were saved, back-sliders restored, and believers sanctified. Praise the Lord ! "
And here is an excerpt from the Lowestoft Diary : " The prayer meetings were charged with power. It is a joy to have Brother Jack Ward witnessing in his own town where he was converted through our witness two years ago. He is now a student, and is here on trek as part of the team, as our cook, musician and soloist. What blessing and inspiration comes

each night as he and Brother Warren sing the appeal !

" The Rev. Charles McCarthy, himself an old Cliff man, loyally stands by us. The evening crowd is always waiting there for us.

" It is a joy to have the help of Lieutenant Campbell and the Girls' Life Brigade. Last year they came out for Christ. Since then they have formed a Cliff Fellowship Prayer Meeting in their church at Sydenham. They have helped tremendously this year, and are keen for spiritual things.

" The Rev. Colin Roberts, the Chairman of the District, also an old Cliff man, joined us for the concluding rally in Lorne Park Road Church, and he delivered a mighty appeal, resulting in the communion-rail being overcrowded with people making a full surrender."

.   .   .   .

How I wish I had space to quote freely from the literature of gratitude.

Here is a letter from one of five men who yielded their lives to Christ one night on the slipway at Morecambe. He is witnessing nobly in his home-town now.

A minister who had heard the team at Bridlington writes : " Those boys have something I had not, and I know many other ministers who would give much to have that something."

A young lady who had wandered from Christ, tells how she prolonged her holiday in order to find a way of restoration ; and then returned home to win her workmates for Christ.

A ship's wireless operator bears witness that the Christ who saved him at Douglas is keeping him all over the world.

Several say that the influence of the campaigns led to new types of Christian service.

Another writes : " No one can tabulate the good done— visitors and townspeople sought Christ ; others experienced a deepening of their spiritual life and went back to their own churches refreshed and strengthened for further effort. Some visitors never missed a meeting during the whole fortnight's holiday.

" Cliff is doing a fine piece of work in training and sending out men filled with the joy of Christianity and an urge to pass on to others what they have found."

XIV

TOLD ROUND THE CAMP FIRE

DURING the first week of August each year, we hold the Derwent Convention at Cliff. It is a big gathering of keen evangelicals, mainly young people, who meet for three purposes—(1) To learn how to study the Bible, (2) To explore the promise of constant spiritual triumph for every believer, (3) To further world-evangelization.

Last August for the first time, we held a Camp for young men in connection with the Convention. It was an amazing success and scores of young men found the secret of The Victorious Life.

One of the best-loved items in the Campers programme was the camp-fire meeting late at night, when we sang the songs of Zion.

It was at one of these meetings that Tony Tilston, one of our number, told us his story. We shall never forget it.

On the evening of St. Leger Day, 1935, the Cliff Trekkers were conducting an evangelistic meeting among the race crowds on Doncaster Market Place. Some of the tipsters were already plying their roguery. One of the fraternity, Tony himself, who had come late, was scouting for the main chance to draw a crowd.

He must do something to recoup his losses. Though he had given four winners of the minor races in the morning, he had fancied Flash By for the big race, and backed it heavily himself ; but Flash By came in last, and Tony lost all the morning takings, as well as fifteen pounds which his father-in-law had asked him to put on another horse. He must get it back somehow. But first he must rake up a crowd. How ? Well, why not heckle the evangelists ?

Happy thought ! Tony stuck the paper under his arm and pushed his way through the religious crowd. T. F. Wilson was speaking, telling them what Christ can do for any man who will give Him a chance. Tony put on a sarcastic grin, and, when the evangelist quietened, bawled out : " Will Jesus Christ put a loaf of bread on my table, mister ? "

Quick as lightning, Stanley Belcher, who was photographing the crowd from the roof of his Gospel car, replied, " Well, since He's sent me four cars, one after another, I think He might manage a loaf of bread for you." Two minutes later Belcher was listening to Tony's story.

The son of drunken parents, he began his education in a ragged school, from which he " graduated " to an industrial school, just after his mother ran away with another man. At sixteen, a hard case, he was sent to farm service, from which he absconded to join the Army. Twice he deserted and re-enlisted. He was court-martialled in France, and suffered field-punishment.

After the War, he took to crime in earnest. He lived by his wits, as card-sharper, thief and pickpocket. Once he sharped his way to America and back. In 1922 he was sentenced to six months' imprisonment for theft and assault upon a policeman. Other sentences followed in various parts of the land. After three months in Wandsworth Gaol, the Prisoner's Aid Society got him a good job on a boat, which he deserted. In 1933, he was arrested for receiving stolen property. The judge described him as " a rogue and the leader of a dangerous gang of thieves," and sentenced him to nine months' imprisonment. After this, Tony decided to be more " respectable " and became a tipster.

The new game was not so dangerous, and paid much better. It was a bad day when Tony took less than ten pounds. He took anything from fifteen to fifty pounds on Grand National Sunday, anything from twenty to sixty pounds on Derby Day, and once, during Ascot Week, he made one hundred and twelve pounds. He did well and became one of the best known racing tipsters in England ; but he was still the sort to stick at nothing. He still carried the handy razor.

.   .   .   .

Tony sold no tips that night on Doncaster Market Place ; and at the end he had not even the price of a bed, so he went with the Trekkers to sleep on the floor of a Methodist Schoolroom. But there was no sleep till Tony was a new man in Christ Jesus.

It is very moving to hear him tell the story of how it happened. One phrase of Wilson's haunted him—" Jesus

Saves." " Will He save me ? " he asked again and again. " He will," answered the Trekkers with tremendous conviction. At last they all knelt together and, when the way of salvation had been explained, Tony prayed for himself : " Jesus Christ, if there is such a Person, make me a different man." The response surprised the suppliant. " I surrendered myself to Him to save me if He could, and he did it ; and from that day to this, He has proved Himself a wonderful Saviour to me."

During that night Tony found both the Saviour and the Gospel. Next morning, he took his stand as usual, and, except that the nucleus was a group of evangelists, drew the usual crowd. Imagine the amazement of the fans when, instead of the usual " special wire," he chalked on the board these words : " My Tip for To-day—Jesus Saves ! " They hardly knew how to take it. It was either a blasphemous joke or a real miracle.

Tony soon solved the problem for them. Very simply and humbly he addressed the crowd : " I'm sorry for any of you that I cheated yesterday. I can't repay. I'm broke. Forgive me. Since yesterday, Jesus Christ has saved me, made me a different man. I'm goin' home to-day to begin a new life. God bless you."

Frank Boynton paid Tony's fare, and put him on the Liverpool train ; then he wired Tony's wife requesting her to meet her changed husband at Lime Street Station. I would like to know what they said to each other on the way to the old home. The task of reorganizing life to suit the Lord Christ must have looked insuperable.

.   .   .   .

Instead of waiting for temptation, Tony immediately sought out the minister of the famous Linacre Mission, himself a former Cliff student.

As they sat together at supper in the manse, Tony, full of his new-found joy, told the minister about that saving crisis at Doncaster.

The minister's first task was to get the new convert in fellowship with understanding believers. They have quite a few at the Linacre Mission who began as Tony did, and, having found salvation in Jesus, have continued with Him into saint-hood. Tony was introduced to them. One of his best pals now is " Happy George," known on the dockside thirty years ago as " Mad Mullah ". Tap-room singer and dancer then ; now one of those who bear witness in the new song. The once " terror " of his wife and children as well as of the neighbourhood is honoured now even by his old companions.

In this fellowship, Tony became established in the Christian Life, began to witness, and was helped through those radical adjustments of life which Christ demands. Everything was different now, especially his home life.

In a little while Tony wrote to his friends at Cliff, " We have a nice little home now, with garden front and back. And Jesus is here ; so it's Heaven. Do you wonder that I have a warm spot in my heart for you Cliff fellows who led me to Christ ? "

.   .   .   .

As soon as he was saved, Tony wanted to tell others of the saving grace of Christ ; and especially he longed to preach the Gospel to racing crowds. But he was woefully ignorant and inadequate. Then Cliff offered to help him.

Although he was forty years of age when he entered Cliff— twice the average age of his fellow-students—and although he had never done five minutes serious study in his life, Tony settled to work with a will. He determined to know the Word of God, even if he broke his health over it, and he did in the end.

Some of the phrases of his testimony come back to me as I write—" I was hated and I hated, but now God has put love in my heart instead. Once I carried a razor in this breast pocket always ready for use on slightest provocation ; now in the same pocket I carry my Bible, the Word of God which is ' sharper than a two-edged sword '." It was worth a good deal to the students of that session to have amongst them a living witness to miraculous conversion.

Tony perhaps gained more from the fellowship than from the lectures. Anyhow, he gave us a mild suggestion that perhaps he was too old to gain much from systematic study. All the same, he went out from Cliff an able and convincing advocate of saving grace ; and upon every opportunity he thanks God for Cliff, not only because it led him to Christ, but also because it taught him how to witness effectively.

After Cliff, Tony became an evangelist. Now, he preaches salvation at race meetings, and in the intervals finds the biggest crowds available elsewhere ; and everywhere he has wonderful power with people who generally spurn the efforts of evangelists. Here are two recent newspaper cuttings—the first from the front page of *The North Mail* on : " The Tipster who Repented."

" Tipster at the racecourse for years, Tony yelled, ' You should be ashamed of yourselves,' as the huge Gosforth Park crowd tensely watched the horses come into the straight on the last lap of the Northumberland Plate yesterday.

" People turned round, annoyed—then rubbed their eyes. The last time they had seen Tony was in 1935, when he sold them winners—and losers.

" One of the best-known racing tipsters had become an evangelist. Standing on a soap-box, Tony lectured them, ' Make peace with your God.'

" Later, Tony told me about himself.

" Since the War he had taken hundreds of pounds from people in sixpenny tips. 'All bluff and personality,' he said. ' You pick your tips out of the morning paper and print them on paper from an exercise book.'

" One day he sold four winners in Doncaster Market Place before the St. Leger Meeting. That night the words of a nearby evangelist drummed in his ears.

" The following morning, crowds turned up to buy his tips. On his board they read : ' My Tip for To-day—Jesus Saves.'

" He has since travelled the country, telling of his conversion at fairs and race meetings.

" Last night he drew a big crowd at an open-air meeting in the Bigg Market."

The second cutting is from the Porthcawl *Advertiser*, under the heading : Ex-Tipster and Convict preaches the Gospel.

" Porthcawl has been thrilled by the life-story of Tony, the ex-tipster, card-sharper and convict who is at Porthcawl preaching.

" Large crowds have gathered every evening during the past week at ' The Green,' where ' Tony ' (as he has already become known to Porthcawl residents and visitors) and the other members of the mission are holding meetings throughout this month.

" Starting life in a ragged school, Tony ' graduated ' to an industrial school. He had earned his living as a racing tipster and cardsharper—and tells of the time when he ' card-sharped ' his way to America and back. He has been in the Army, was court-martialled and endured field-punishment. He has seen the inside of Wandsworth, Walton and Strangeways prisons, and has been described by the magistrates as ' the leader of a dangerous gang of thieves ! ' His unfailing companion on all occasions was a razor—carried at all times in his breast pocket ! And now Tony holds large crowds spellbound as he shouts out his ' tip for to-day.'

"Smartly dressed residents of Porthcawl's fashionable hotels, gay young people in beach outfits, officers and men from the Territorial camp, and all the other types that frequent Porthcawl's promenade—listen intently as Tony tells them how to find the happiness they are looking for. ' My tip for to-day is—Jesus saves ! ' he tells them with the greatest sincerity and conviction."

.   .   .   .

Cliff inculcates the rule that an evangelist must preach for a verdict every time. Tony does it with astounding success. Here is a typical extract from his bulletin : " You will rejoice to hear that God has mightily blessed my witness, and to know that He is still keeping me in His grace and favour. Wherever I go, it is my privilege to see men and women coming to the Saviour. We had a wonderful meeting last night, and what joy to see eleven men come forward to accept Christ. Last Sunday there were thirty-four seekers."

Time and place make no difference. While he was speaking at the " Grand National " last year, giving the race-going public real " inside information," an American visitor stood to listen. It was afterwards revealed that this man had travelled thousands of miles to see the great race. At the very moment the race was being run he was on his knees seeking Christ, and was led to Him by " Tony the Tipster ". He did not see the race, but he saw the Saviour. And one Sunday soon afterwards, Tony pointed seventeen souls to Christ in a London church.

" If there's anything more I can do to help the Lord's work," says Tony, " here I am, send me." So long as he keeps in that frame of mind, and continues to sign himself " Yours in His grace and favour," God will bless Tony and work life-changing miracles through him.

XV

PROVISION

WHAT of the economics ? How is this work sustained ?
Of the founder of this work, Samuel Chadwick said,
" Thomas Champness was pre-eminently a man of faith. He
lived in the unseen. God was real and nigh at hand. In all
his ventures he took God into his reckoning. That was why
he dared big things and took great risks. He ventured with
God. The Joyful News Mission was a venture of faith. God
had infinite resources, and Thomas Champness was His
servant. He did not go at his own charges, God Almighty
backed his undertakings. In times of difficulty he went to
God. A rich man said to him one day : ' Champness, if ever
you are in want of money, let me know.' Mr. Champness
replied ' When I want money, I shall never tell you, but you
will know.' God was his banker."

Thomas Champness made no collections, issued no appeals,
and received no connexional grants. " We have no resources
but in God, to Whom all the silver and the gold belong.
Through the favour of His people He meets all our needs, and
so long as He wants the work done by us, He will see to
supplies." That was his boast and he was not confounded.

The financial basis remains unchanged, except that two
ministers on the staff are now maintained from Connexional
funds. Each student is expected to contribute according to his
ability ; there have never been any fees. A few contribute
the whole cost, many give a little and others nothing. But no
man is accepted because he can pay ; and no man is declined
because he is poor. No distinction is made. The test is calling,
not means ; and Cliff has always been the College of the
Unprivileged.

Cliff depends upon free gifts ; that explains the romance of
its upkeep. It has a few friends among the rich, who have
gained strength from its witness and in return give from their
abundance ; but the main support of Cliff is the favour of the
common people, chiefly readers of *The Joyful News*, who give

92

out of their poverty. We have scores of heart-moving stories of their sacrifices for this work's sake.

The supreme example of the confidence of the common people in Cliff is the anniversary every Whitsuntide.

On Whit-Monday there are excursions to Cliff from every corner of the land, bringing sometimes up to fifteen thousand people for a season of Pentecostal witness and song. The greatest evangelists in the world foregather for the occasion ; and revival services continue all day. There are wonderful scenes of conversion and consecration. It is a festival of evangelism, a great love-feast, in the original Methodist spirit, on national lines.

I remember how deeply impressed I was by my first experience of the anniversary gatherings. All sorts of questions arose in my mind. How is it to be explained ? What means this eager, anxious throng ? It must be the most remarkable gathering of its kind in Britain. How shall we account for it ?

My own answers to these questions had profound influence upon me. At the lowest level that multitude meant widespread interest in Cliff. Yet it was not interest alone that brought them. Scores of these people were led to Cliff by deep desire. There is no mistake about it ; many came to find the secret of victorious living. It had been noised abroad that " God is in this place " ; and yearning, earnest, seeking souls come hither " if peradventure they might find Him " in saving or sanctifying grace. At every meeting, and through every waking hour, there were seekers.

There was something more. I said within myself : These people feel the desperate need of Revival. They see the tragic futility of the common piety. They are weary of a Christianity without force or effect. They have realized that we shall never be able to establish the Kingdom of God among the nations till there has been a tremendous strengthening of evangelical life and faith. . . . They want another Evangelical Revival, and they know that it can never come till we return from the distant outskirts to the central verities of the Christian Faith, for which Cliff stands.

What means this eager, anxious throng ? Simply a multitude of believers who believe in the Need and Promise of Evangelical Faith and gather together one day annually to affirm their faith, confirm their hope, and strengthen their mutual devotion.   That answer influenced me profoundly.

But there is something else : They came to Cliff to GIVE. The wonder of the anniversary is the collection.   It is not organized for money-raising, but the people come to give, and from faith in Cliff and love for its work, they give with abandon and joy.   The offertory is a genuine thankoffering of the thousands who believe in our Gospel and love our work. The collection regularly exceeds three thousand pounds.

They give at the anniversary ; and they give again and again afterwards.   Before God, in the Spirit of sacred trust, we translate the gifts into soul-saving enterprise.

The work goes on in triumph because God continues to answer the prayer of faith through the generosity of His servants.   We set to our seal that God is faithful.   Of all the good gifts promised to Thomas Champness sixty years ago, not one hath failed.   And we share Champness' conviction, " Through the favour of His people, He meets all our needs, and so long as He wants the work done by us, He will see to the supplies."